CAUGHT IN THE CRISIS

CAUGHT IN THE CRISIS

Women and the U.S. Economy Today

TERESA AMOTT

MONTHLY REVIEW PRESS
NEW YORK

Copyright © 1993 by Teresa Amott
All rights reserved

Library of Congress Cataloging-in-Publication Data
Amott, Teresa L.
  Caught in the crisis : women and the U.S. economy today / by Teresa Amott.
    p. cm. — (Cornerstone books)
  Includes bibliographical references.
  ISBN 0-85345-845-6 (cloth) : $22.00. — ISBN 0-85345-846-4 (paper) : $10.00
  1. Women—Employment—United States. 2. Women—United States—
Economic conditions. I. Title. II. Cornerstone books (New York, N.Y.)
HD6095.A664 1993
331.4'0973—dc20   93-7326
                                            CIP

Monthly Review Press
122 West 27th Street
New York, NY 10001

Manufactured in the United States of America
10   9   8   7   6   5   4   3   2   1

CONTENTS

CONTENTS

ACKNOWLEDGMENTS

All writing is a social process, and this book is no exception. Most of my written work over the past fourteen years has been a collaborative effort with my friend Julie Matthaei. This time, however, Julie and her partner were busy sharing their lives with a new baby, Ella. I have missed Julie's companionship and intellectual stimulation, particularly since so many of the book's central concepts were born during our work in the past. Chapter 1 in particular is in large measure an updated restatement of Chapters 9 and 10 of our book *Race, Gender, and Work: A Multicultural Economic History of Women in the U.S. Economy,* which we published in 1991. It is to acknowledge the central, although invisible, role that Julie has played in this current work that I dedicate it to Ella. I also dedicate it to my companion Ernie, whose extraordinary support was essential throughout.

The editing skill of Susan Lowes, Director of Monthly Review Press, rescued the book from economic jargon. Most remarkable was her patience, as the demands of my teaching schedule at Bucknell translated into one delay after another. Many people read drafts, including Julie, Ernie, Sarah Pryor, Brenda Smeeton, Paul Susman, and Jill Szafranski, and their comments shaped the book in important ways, although they are of course not responsible for any errors that remain. Sarah and Brenda created the graphs and checked the references. With amazing good humor, they looked up missing citations, followed vague directions, accomodated themselves to my schedule, and learned the mysteries of graphics, spreadsheets, and indexes. They also served as the first editors, reading every word and providing invaluable comments. This book is in a real sense meant for them: for today's students and activists who want to understand and change the world.

1

WOMEN AND ECONOMIC CRISIS

When the economy slows down, people get hurt. For the most vulnerable, a slowdown in economic growth can lead to unemployment, bankruptcy, poverty, and even homelessness. The cost to individual men and women is staggering. Heart attacks, mental illness, domestic violence, crime, and suicide all increase when unemployment rises.[1] Other effects are less dramatic but still affect people's day-to-day lives. Leisure time vanishes when people have to work longer hours to keep from falling behind, worry and insecurity take their toll on human relationships, young people have to lower their aspirations while parents' dreams for their children fade. Since women bear much of the burden of maintaining family life, they are particularly hard hit by the less quantifiable costs of economic crisis. But because much of women's work is both unnoticed and unpaid—or underappreciated and underpaid—it is difficult to measure these costs. Four examples, taken from the lives of four real women, illustrate these issues.

Ina Mae Best is one of the casualties of the crisis. At age fifty-one and after eighteen years of excellent work, she was fired from her job in a textile factory because she supported a union organizing drive. Best went to work at Goldtex, Inc., in eastern North Carolina, after her youngest son started school. When union organizers arrived, they asked questions that made Best begin to wonder about her working conditions: Why had her salary increased only $2 in eighteen years? Why did the supervisors treat the workers as though they were less than human? Why did the company lie to the workers about its profits, claiming that they were too small to permit better wages? But when Best began to raise these issues, she was dismissed. The risk of losing your job for union activity grew in the 1980s, as the government agency charged with enforcing labor rules supported management over the workers.[2]

Glenda Schmidt is another casualty of the crisis. A thirty-nine-year-old mother of five in Marshalltown, Iowa, Schmidt earns less than $6 an hour as a part-time nurse's aide. Her employer calls her in to work only when she is needed, so she cannot count on a steady income every week. Until October 1991, she had received welfare benefits and Medicaid, the government-sponsored health care plan that provides free care to poor families. Schmidt needs medication for hypertension, migraine headaches, and stomach problems, and the medication for her youngest child's kidney disease costs $180 a month. But Schmidt and her family face a Catch-22 situation: her job does not provide health benefits, but in most months her earnings are too high for the family to qualify for Medicaid. Before 1981, Schmidt would have been able to keep her Medicaid coverage, but regulations enacted by the Reagan administration took away health benefits from thousands of working women like Schmidt.[3]

Felipa Perez, a sewing machine operator in an El Paso, Texas, factory found herself in jail in 1991 as a result of the economic crisis. Her employer closed down, owing Perez and other workers weeks of back pay, and then started up again under another name. To dramatize their situation, Perez and five other women chained themselves to sewing machines in the new factory, and were carted off to jail by the police. A mother of four, Perez had never imagined that she would be arrested. Yet during the 1980s, over 5,000 jobs were lost in El Paso's garment industry when factories closed and moved across the border to Mexico. The Department of Labor, which was supposed to ensure that the workers were treated fairly when their plants shut down, ignored the plight of Perez and women like her.[4]

While the economic crisis led to enormous suffering, a few women prospered. For instance, Linda J. Wachner, the only female chief executive of a Fortune 500 company, became the richest working woman in the United States. Starting as department store buyer in 1974, Wachner's salary catapulted into the stratosphere in 1986 when she led a takeover of Warnaco, Inc., which makes lingerie and men's sportswear. In 1990, she earned $2.5 million in salary and bonuses, even though the company posted *losses* of over $28 million.[5] Analysts estimate Wachner's net worth at $100 million.

These stories illustrate that the effects of economic crisis are complicated and varied. Not all women have been affected in the same way because not all women are the same. Class, racial-ethnicity, sexual orientation, age, and family status (married, divorced, never married, with or without children) all play crucial roles in shaping women's choices and in structuring their opportunities. The chapters that follow investigate the effects of the economic crisis on women, trace the forces that have changed their lives, and examine the ways in which they have resisted these forces, taking the initiative to protest unfairness and fight for change. How have women fared during these years of slow growth, high unemployment, declining standards of living, and increasing inequality between rich and poor?

We also look at the larger picture, because we need to understand the causes of the crisis. Why did the long economic boom that had produced higher standards of living for every successive generation in the United States since World War II come to a grinding halt in the 1970s? What was the human cost of this crisis? Who bore the burden? Most important, what can be done to alleviate the pain and end the crisis?

Because this history is so important, the rest of this chapter is devoted to a brief overview of the development of women's economic roles until the beginning of the economic crisis, focusing on the development of economic and social hierarchies that have created differences *and* similarities among women of different racial-ethnic groups and classes. Chapter 2 looks at the nature of the economic crisis itself.

The following three chapters focus on the effects of the crisis on women in three arenas: wage work, the household and the government. Chapter 3 looks at women in different occupations to see how the crisis has affected their wages, working conditions, and opportunities for advancement. Chapter 4 traces the effects of the crisis on women as members of families and households, focusing on the increased burdens of unpaid work in the home. Finally, Chapter 5 surveys the effects of conservative policies on health, job safety, child care, and welfare.

WOMEN'S ROLES IN THE ECONOMY

Women workers play a dual role in capitalist economies such as our own, producing commodities (goods and services offered for sale on the market) on the job, which economists call *production*, and caring for themselves and their families in the home, referred to as *reproduction*. Most women have to work in both these arenas and therefore work a "double day": they work for wages in the labor market and work without pay in the home.[6]

Before capitalism became the dominant economic system in the United States, women's work was not so clearly split between these two arenas. In an earlier book, Julie Matthaei and I noted how women's work lives have changed, in part because of the huge influx of immigrant labor:

> In the last five centuries, Native Americans have been joined by millions of immigrant women and men of diverse racial-ethnic and economic backgrounds. These immigrants came—some voluntarily, others at gunpoint—into a variety of different economic niches, including slavery, indentured servitude, contract labor, self-employment, and wage work. The United States expanded across Mexico and incorporated Puerto Rico, the Philippines, and Hawaii. And a fledgling economic system of profit-motivated production for the market, based on wage labor, grew into the dominant economic and social force determining women's work lives, not only in the United States, but in the world.[7]

If we look carefully at those five centuries, we see that women's economic roles, like those of men, have been affected by a number of social categories, the most important of which are gender, race or ethnicity, and class. (While other social categories, including age, sexual orientation, and religion, have been enormously important, they are not my focus here.) In our society, people identify themselves partly in terms of each of these three categories, however they understand them. But these categories of identity are socially defined, not biologically determined: we may, for instance, associate gender differences with physical differences, but that does not mean that gender differences are necessarily related to biological differences. Even though only women can physically bear children, they need not be the sole caretakers. It is our patterns of socialization, customs, and social institutions that have led us to turn the *physical* ability to bear children into a *social* role as the primary caregiver. Sex has to do with biological differences; gender has to do with social differences. Gender roles have changed enormously in the twentieth century—for instance, most mothers are now employed outside the home—but the vast differences that remain between the lives of women and men mean that gender is still a crucial social category.

Race and ethnicity are also far less connected to biology than many people believe. At the molecular level, there are no differences between people that make one group into a *race*, and yet race and ethnicity (based on country of origin) are two of the most important social categories in the United States today.[8] Most of our institutions are structured in ways that privilege whites over people of color, so that race and ethnicity continue to play an enormous role in our lives.

Finally, class is another important social category. Class has been defined by social scientists in many different ways. Here I will use a definition derived from the Marxist tradition and define each class by its relationship to the ways in which society provides for its material needs. Usually, one *class* of people organizes production because it owns the means of production—the machinery, factories, office buildings, and other property that make production possible. Because of its dominant economic role, this owning class has enormous power over all areas of social life, including the government. In the feudal system, which preceded capitalism in Western Europe, the land-owning *nobility* directed the production of the *serfs* who worked the land. In the United States today, *capitalists* own the means of production, while *workers*, although they vary in pay, status, and working conditions, all lack access to ownership of these important means of production.

All of the social categories that we have been discussing— gender, race-ethnicity, and class—are interconnected and are part of what defines the experiences of different groups of people. For instance, the experiences of white women have been different from those of white men *and* from those of African American women. Their uniqueness lies at the *intersection* of race and gender, the ways in which being white makes their experience of womanhood different from the experience of other women, and the ways in which being a woman makes their experience of whiteness different from the experience of white men.

Now let us turn to a brief overview of the development of the U.S. economy, always keeping in mind the need to examine the ways in which all these social categories intersect if we are to understand people's experiences. When we do this, we shall see that the economy developed in ways that gave different groups of people different roles according to the gender, race-ethnicity, and class categories to which they belonged.

BEFORE WAGE LABOR

As late as the mid-1800s, many different types of economic systems coexisted in the United States, including family farming, the *hacienda* system of large ranches in the Southwest, plantation slavery in the South, the economies of the different Native American nations, and the early capitalist industrial enterprises.[9] Each was characterized by a particular form of labor, or *labor-system*—by the way in which work got done and by the class that owned and controlled the means of production. Race and ethnicity played a central role in determining which people were assigned to which labor system, while gender and class determined in large measure what work people performed as part of the system.

Take the example of the family system, which was where most European Americans were to be found. Here husbands, wives, and children worked together in a business or on a farm that was a self-sufficient unit of economic life. Sometimes the labor of family members was supplemented by that of indentured servants—men and women who, in exchange for room, board, and passage from Europe, were required to work for their masters for a certain number of years. At the end of the term, these indentured servants were "free," although the conditions of their bondage were sometimes so harsh that they did not survive long enough to enjoy their freedom.[10] Self-sufficient family production was also common for free African Americans and some Puerto Rican, Chicano, and Asian families.

Even though the members of these families worked together, the men exercised enormous power over their wives and children, directing their labor and representing them in political life (women were not allowed to vote until a constitutional amendment was ratified in 1920). The goods and services produced under this system were generally consumed by the family itself, but surpluses were taken to market and sold for cash.

The plantation system was different. Here white owners bought black slaves and forced them to work at agricultural labor for free. The slave system was supported by repression and violence, both of which were legally sanctioned in order to protect the property rights of the slaveowners. Female slaves had a dual role: they worked in the fields and homes of the slaveowners, and they also reproduced wealth by bearing slave children, often as a consequence of rape at the hands of white men.[11]

The *hacienda* system, common in the Southwest, involved large landowners of Spanish origin and *péon* families of *mestizo* (American Indian and Spanish) origin. The *péons* were permitted to engage in small-scale agricultural production for their families, but most of their time was devoted to working for the landowner. Unlike slaves, *péons* were legally free, but in practice they could not move off the *hacienda* and often remained there for generations. Women worked the fields and raised the children, but rarely participated in large-scale commercial activities on the *hacienda*, such as ranching.

Prior to the invasion of European settlers, different Native American nations engaged in their own self-sufficient economic activities. Some farmed, while others hunted, fished, or trapped. Women's work depended on the predominant form of economic activity, and often involved an important religious role as well. As the white settlers overran the Native Americans' lands, their way of life was destroyed, and by the late 1800s most Native Americans had been pushed onto reservations far from their original lands, their self-sufficient economic systems utterly destroyed.

Beginning in the late 1600s, the capitalist system—in which a capitalist hired workers for a wage and sold the goods and services they produced in a market—began to gather momentum. Capitalism differed from the family system that had preceded it in a number of ways. First, the capitalist was not engaged in self-sufficient production for his own family's needs. (I say *his* because early capitalists were almost always white men. There were many reasons for this, including the political disenfranchisement and ban on property ownership for white married women and all people of color, and social norms that confined women to the home.) Second, instead of producing a range of different goods and services, the capitalist focused on one particular market. Third, capitalists hired workers instead of depending on slaves or *péons*. They were able to harness new technologies and mass production techniques, breaking each task into several parts so that no one worker or group of workers was skilled in all aspects of the job. Not only did this make workers easier to train, but it made them easier to control. The first factories to use these new production techniques developed in the Northeast, and the first industrial workers in the United States were farmers' daughters who spun cotton and fleece into cloth for sale in the market.

THE GROWTH OF WAGE LABOR

Beginning in the early 1800s, people were slowly drawn into industrial wage work. In 1780, only one in six residents (not including Native Americans) was a wage worker or indentured servant; the rest were either self-employed or slaves. By 1890, only one hundred years later, two out of three were wage workers.[12] But people from different racial-ethnic groups entered the wage labor force at different rates. The first were the European Americans, who moved from owning their own farms and businesses or from indentured servitude. These formerly independent farmers and craftworkers were stripped of their independence and skills, displaced by capitalists who could produce the same commodities in greater quantities and sell them for less. The immigrants who arrived from Europe in the second half of the nineteenth century also became wage workers. Married women generally stayed at home, while single women, children, and men joined the factory workforce or became domestic servants.

But African Americans were barred from wage labor for decades longer. Long after the Emancipation Proclamation of 1863, most African Americans remained in agriculture, sharecropping, or tenant farming. African American women became domestic servants. Not until the labor shortages created by World War I and World War II did large numbers of African Americans enter the industrial labor force.

Other racial-ethnic groups also entered the industrial workforce later. Chicanos and Chicanas entered the wage labor force in the latter half of the nineteenth century, and were predominantly domestic servants, garment workers, and migrant farm workers.[13] Asian Americans arrived during the nineteenth century to do contract work on plantations, railroads, farms, or brothels, but anti-Asian sentiment barred them from factory wage labor until World War II. As a result, some Asians set up family farms and small businesses, while others struggled to find migrant or seasonal work. Women typically worked in the family business. Native Americans remained outside the wage labor force until very recently. Confined to reservations where jobs were scarce, most eked out a living through farming, craft work, and odd jobs.

WOMEN'S ENTRY INTO THE WAGE LABOR FORCE

In each of these groups, single women, children, and men—both married and single—entered the wage labor force before married women. From 1830 to 1930, most married women of all racial-ethnic groups did not work outside the home. Powerful economic and social forces reinforced these wives' dependency on their husbands. Not only was the wage earned by the average man far higher than that earned by the average woman, but the primitive conditions of the nineteenth century home or tenement made homemaking a full-time job:

> One researcher estimated that in poor urban households in the 1840s and 1850s, the money a homemaker saved her family by scavenging, bargain shopping, caring for her own children, doing her own housecleaning, and taking in boarders or performing odd jobs was more than double what she could have earned in the formal, paid labor force. Freed Black women especially sought to avoid wage work, since domesticity [remaining in the home, outside the wage labor force] allowed them to escape the racial and sexual exploitation of a white master or mistress and enabled them to devote time and energy to their own children.[14]

Finally, traditions of male power and authority confined women to the domestic sphere, where they could be supervised closely by their male relatives. Wives stayed home to do the unpaid reproductive work that enabled the family to survive, while their husbands sought to earn a wage high enough so that they could keep their wives out of the labor force. In poor immigrant families, it was often child labor that supplemented men's earnings so that the wives remained in the home.

Even the labor shortage created by World War I failed to push many married women into the labor force, although it did provide opportunities for some. The war also opened up opportunities for many African Americans, millions of whom migrated north to escape from the faltering agricultural economy of the South. As they came north, the men found jobs in manufacturing, particularly in the most dangerous and underpaid factory work, while most women worked as domestic servants.

The postwar boom of the 1920s provided more opportunities, and women began to move more rapidly into the workforce—particularly white women, both married and single. As women left the home, more and more of the unpaid work of homemaking came to be "commoditized"—families ate out in restaurants, clothing was bought "off the rack," and leisure activities came to rely more and more on purchased goods (such as television). Families needed more and more cash income to purchase the goods and services that they no longer produced at home. The culture of consumerism expanded needs, and women entered the workforce to help fill these needs.

But unpaid work in the household did not disappear. Rising standards of living led to rising standards of homemaking. For instance, the introduction of the vacuum cleaner actually led to an *increase* in the amount of time women spent cleaning their homes, since floors now had to be clean enough to eat off![15] In addition, some aspects of the reproductive work of the family proved resistant to commoditization, partly because men insisted on the personal service of their wives. For these and other reasons, which we will explore in more detail in Chapter 4, the burden of the "double day" intensified.

Women continued to move into the labor force. During the Great Depression of the 1930s, households needed to replace the wages lost by unemployed husbands, fathers, and brothers—in fact, during the Depression women's overall unemployment rates were lower than men's. But work in the home intensified still further as women sewed, canned, and baked in order to conserve cash by replacing store-bought goods with those made at home.

It is often said that World War II led to a huge upswing in women's participation in the wage labor force. But while it is true that many women found jobs in war industries, the trend had been established well before the war, as we have seen. In fact, over three-quarters of the women who held paid jobs during the war had worked before. The big differences were the participation of married women and the possibility of holding high-paying jobs that had once been considered "men's work."[16] Such gains were only temporary, however, and immediately after the war women were pushed out of men's jobs when the popular media launched a campaign to return them to their "traditional" roles as wives and homemakers. Many women left the labor force, while others, who remained at work, were pushed out of men's jobs and confined to stereotypically female occupations.

During the 1950s and 1960s, the economy entered a long period of growth that economists refer to as the postwar boom, which lasted until the early 1970s. Married women of all racial-ethnic groups were drawn into the economy during these decades of growth, joining single women in a range of women's jobs. Clerical work expanded dramatically, as did such women's professions as teaching, library work, and nursing.

LABOR MARKET HIERARCHIES

Although the increase in workforce participation led to an increase in women's financial independence as more and more women became able to count on an income of their own, there were still large economic disparities between men and women. The explanation of this paradox lies in the way in which the labor market had been structured hierarchically by gender and by race-ethnicity from the earliest years of U.S. history:

> As white women and people of color entered the labor market from other labor systems, they found themselves engaged in a struggle for earnings and power in which they were at a disadvantage. Employers commonly used them as a low-wage labor force, often as replacements for or strikebreakers against existing workers. The threatened workers, usually white and/or male, fought to defend their jobs by attacking these less powerful workers.[17]

As different groups of people entered the labor force at different times, they were channeled into some jobs and excluded from others. For example, during the nineteenth century labor unions dominated by white men helped pass legislation to prevent women from holding certain types of jobs, such as those requiring heavy lifting or night work. During the Great Depression, many cities passed laws that barred married women from jobs as schoolteachers so that these jobs would be reserved for men. Sometimes the process of exclusion was violent, as when white workers rioted to prevent employers from hiring African Americans or Asians. All these different mechanisms—some legal, some not—helped establish and enforce a hierarchy of sex and race in the labor force by reserving certain jobs for white men and confining women and men of color to the jobs that remained.

In the 1960s, movements to dismantle these hierarchies began to grow. The civil rights movement sought to tear down the legal barriers to African American advancement in education and jobs. Affirmative action programs and the movement for school integration led race barriers in a number of occupations to fall. By 1970, for instance, large numbers of African American women were working outside domestic service. The women's liberation movement of the early 1970s, drawing strength, inspiration, and tactics from the civil rights movement, set into motion the gradual dismantling of the barriers to women's entry into a number of occupations. Both movements were possible in part because of the postwar economic boom, which led to the creation of new jobs and a high demand for workers.

But both these movements also met stiff opposition from white men who sought to protect their privileged position in the workplace. While a few members of previously discriminated against groups have moved one or two rungs up the ladder, the labor market hierarchy itself remains firmly in place. Most women remain confined to stereotypically female jobs, where wages and opportunities for advancement are low. Most racial-ethnic minorities are confined to low-wage jobs. White men continue to hold the most highly paid, prestigious jobs and continue to own and control most of the nation's wealth.

WOMEN ON THE EVE OF THE CRISIS

In 1970, as the economy was poised on the brink of economic crisis, 42.6 percent of white women, 49.5 percent of African American women, and 39.3 percent of Latinas were officially counted as being "in the workforce"—a statistical category that includes both those who are employed and those who are looking for work. More and more women had incomes of their own, although few earned enough to support their families. Most worked in female-dominated occupations, and discrimination by race or ethnicity further limited their access to jobs. African American women, for instance, were *nine times* more likely to be domestic servants than white women.[18] In 1973, only 8.4 percent of white women, 4.6 percent of African American women, and 3.2 percent of Latinas were college graduates.[19]

The most common form of family, in every racial-ethnic group, was the married couple, and roughly four-fifths of all children lived with two parents. Nevertheless, there were significant differences by race-ethnicity: for instance, African American women of all ages were far more likely to be unmarried than whites or Latinas.

In the next two decades—from 1970 to 1990—women's participation in the labor force increased substantially. New jobs were created, and political organizing awakened a sense of entitlement among both women and racial-ethnic minorities. But women's overall economic situation did not improve dramatically. Had the postwar economic boom continued, life would have been very different for all women, and particularly for women of color. Not only would women have continued to enter the labor force, but household incomes would have grown as well. Instead, women became caught in an economic crisis that affected not only the United States but the entire world: as a result, they received a growing share of a shrinking economic pie. The causes of this crisis, and the ways in which it affected the economy, are the subject of the next chapter.

2

THE POSTWAR ECONOMY SLOWS DOWN

Early in 1992, surveys that asked people about their confidence in the U.S. economy showed a level of anxiety that was unusual for the United States. When they were asked about their outlook on the future, respondents said that the economy would continue to stagnate, that mass layoffs would continue, and that their children were likely to have a lower standard of living than they had had.[1] These fears had been building since the early 1970s, when the economy went haywire: inflation soared, wages stagnated, and unemployment began to rise. The crisis touched everyone, from the highest paid executive to the counter-worker at McDonald's. The difference was that those at the top saw their incomes soar to unprecedented levels, while the average worker struggled to pay the bills.

WHAT IS AN ECONOMIC CRISIS?

Although many people say that the U.S. economy is in "crisis," they mean very different things by the term. Some mean a recession, defined by economists as when the production of goods and services fails to grow for more than six months, unemployment rises, and spending falls. Others mean a longer term problem, such as the country's inability to compete internationally or the persistence of huge federal budget deficits. In this book, the term is used to mean a very specific problem that capitalist economies experience periodically, when economic growth—the ability of the economy to produce more and more goods and services—slows down for a protracted period, producing serious political as well as economic problems. A structural crisis grows out of the specific nature of capitalism: the very dynamic that leads to economic expansion can turn on itself and lead to stagnation. The last such crisis was the Great Depression of the 1930s. Between the 1940s and the early 1970s, the world economy emerged from this crisis and entered a period of prolonged expansion. Then, in the early 1970s, production slowed in all the industrial economies—from an annual growth in the value of goods and services of 5 percent in the 1960s to 3.5 percent in the 1970s.[2]

One reason that capitalist economies don't fail all the time is that there are institutions that help prop up the system, promoting expansion and (only temporarily) delaying the onset of a crisis. These institutions include the financial system, the political system, and the family system. In a structural crisis, most of these are called into question as the society struggles to restore growth. The capitalist economy therefore emerges from a structural crisis significantly changed, as new institutions emerge and old ones are restructured in order to facilitate another boom.

THE ROOTS OF THE CRISIS

Like all economic crises, the crisis that began in the 1970s had its roots in the long expansionary period that preceded it. Writing in 1982, economists Jim Campen and Arthur Mac-Ewan identified three important factors that supported and facilitated this boom: U.S. hegemony (dominance) abroad, the capital-labor accord (a period of relative labor peace), and an activist government committed to maintaining demand for goods and services.[3]

World War II cemented the role of the United States as the dominant world power, economically and militarily. The nation was able to dictate terms to other countries that ensured it access to raw materials and markets, and protected U.S. business interests abroad.[4] It pumped huge sums of foreign aid into Europe and Japan to repair their war-torn economies—so that they could then buy U.S. products and provide attractive investment opportunities for U.S. companies. U.S. corporations set up operations across the globe, assured that the military and political might of the government would protect their investments and assured that foreigners would be able to purchase their goods.

A second element of the postwar boom involved an uneasy truce between "big labor"—the large industrial unions that represented most of the country's manufacturing workers—and "big business"—the large companies that dominated major industries such as automaking and steel. The terms of the truce were that big business would permit unions to organize and allow wages to grow along with worker productivity. In other words, the corporations would grant workers a share of the growing economic pie. For its part, labor promised not to protest many management decisions that directly affected the workers, such as what technology to introduce and where to locate the plants. This freed employers from the possibility that militant unions would threaten their ability to make profits. Although the majority of white women and racial-ethnic minority workers were not members of the "big labor" unions, and although millions of small businesses remained outside the "big business" sector, a large enough share of business and labor were involved in this informal agreement to provide a period of labor peace that was highly conducive to economic growth.

The Global Economy. "The growth of U.S.-based transnationals has taken its toll on the American labor force. According to estimates by Norman Glickman and Douglas Woodward, foreign investment by U.S. companies has eliminated nearly three million American manufacturing jobs since 1977. These companies now employ more than six million workers abroad.... The most 'globalized' is the auto industry.... Using both subcontractors and plants of its own, General Motors gets, for example, engines from Australia, ignition parts from Singapore, and anti-lock brakes from West Germany. Ford gets transmissions from France, cylinder heads from Italy, and trim from Mexico. Chrysler gets door hinges from South Korea, springs from England, and wheels from Brazil. Moreover, all three companies import entire vehicles from such countries as Japan, Mexico, and South Korea to sell under their name in the U.S."—Philip Mattera, *Prosperity Lost.*[5]

Finally, the postwar period was characterized by an increased willingness on the part of the government to intervene in the economy, particularly by buying goods and services from the private sector. The military was the source of much of this buying—so much so that it accounted for nearly 7 out of every 100 jobs through the 1950s.[6] In addition, the government had created "safety nets" that guaranteed income to retired and unemployed workers, helping to ensure that demand for goods and services would not collapse during periods of economic downturn. The safety net grew after the war, covering more people and offering larger benefits.

But the same factors that helped the economy to grow were to spell the end of the boom, creating increasing problems for U.S. business in the global economy. Economic dominance, for instance, depended on the political domination of third world countries which served as markets for U.S. goods and sources of raw materials for U.S. manufacturers. But in the 1960s, the peoples of these countries began to resist the domination of the advanced capitalist countries. One example was Vietnam, where a national liberation movement fought the U.S. for over a decade, at an enormous cost to both societies; other liberation movements gathered strength across the globe, from Algeria to Guatemala to Indonesia. In addition, the United States had come to count on a steady supply of cheap oil from the third world. The U.S. economy was built on low-cost energy: cheap automobile travel meant that suburbs could grow up around the major cities and industries could ignore (or even suppress) energy-conserving technologies. As a result, the economy was highly vulnerable to any change in the availability or price of oil.

By the early 1970s, the United States had poured millions of dollars and thousands of lives into fighting the Vietnam war. The oil-producing nations had joined together into an organization called OPEC (Organization of Oil-Exporting Countries) and restricted production so sharply that the price of oil doubled, sending the economy into a tailspin.[7] European and Japanese businesses, which possessed newer and more energy-efficient technologies, gained a new advantage over U.S. producers.[8]

In addition, businesses faced problems with rising labor costs. During the boom years, as economic growth created more and more jobs, unemployment rates had fallen steadily (the only exceptions to the trend were a few short periods of recession, always followed by recovery). In the last half of the 1960s, for instance, the unemployment rate was less than 4 percent (see Figure 2-1). Some workers, particularly those in unions, were

Figure 2-1
Unemployment Rate, 1948–1990
(16 years and over)

Detailed sources for all figures can be found on pp. 155–56.

able to take advantage of the relatively low levels of unemployment to win higher wages, more benefits, and better working conditions. Eventually, rising labor costs began to cut into profits.[9] In addition, greater working class power during the postwar boom had led to the expansion of safety net policies that favored workers, including such social welfare programs as social security, welfare, unemployment compensation, Medicare and Medicaid, and food stamps. All of these made workers less dependent on their employers and more able to resist employer demands for cuts in wages.

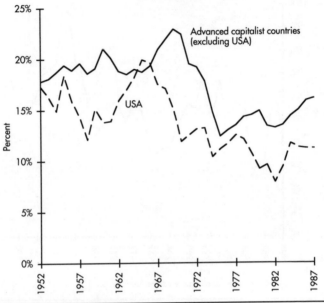

Figure 2-2
Business Net Profit Rate, 1952–1987
(in percent)

THE CORPORATE RESPONSE TO THE CRISIS

In these ways, then, the prolonged economic boom sowed the seeds of its own destruction. But as the profit rate declined dramatically (see Figure 2-2), corporations began to seek ways to reverse the situation. They had four main strategies: (1) to bolster profits by moving operations to lower cost regions of the United States or to other countries; (2) to diminish the power of the workers and their unions; (3) to reorganize the work process to use lower paid and part-time workers; and (4) to lobby the government to pass legislation that would favor their interests, such as changes in environmental laws. Each of these strategies was designed to lower costs and raise profits, thereby restarting the engine of the U.S. business machine.

Capital Flight

Capital flight—when a corporation moves its operation in order to lower its costs—has been a common corporate strategy during the crisis, particularly in manufacturing. In some industries, such as shoes and textiles, capital flight began much earlier, when northern manufacturers moved to low-wage, non-unionized states across the South. Beginning in the 1970s, however, businesses found it increasingly easy to move even further away, taking the jobs overseas and leaving behind boarded-up factories, unemployed workers, depressed cities and towns, and a "deindustrialized" United States.

One factor in the increased rate of capital flight was the new technology of global communications. Once a corporate headquarters in New Jersey could send out style and pattern information to cutting and sewing shops in Haiti or Thailand, the Philippines or the Caribbean, using fax machines and satellite teleconferencing, there was no need to have the factory nearby.

In addition, a change in the attitudes of foreign governments eased the red tape that had discouraged companies headquartered in one country from opening plants in another.[11] At the end of World War II, for instance, many countries had policies that made it difficult for capitalists from other countries to make investments, to hold foreign currencies, to buy land, or to build factories. By the late 1970s, many of these barriers had begun to fall, as the United States became an active promoter of "free trade"—the free movement of both capital and goods from one country to another.[12] At home, U.S. businesses benefitted from a tax code that allowed them to avoid paying U.S. taxes on corporate profits they earned abroad.

Capital Flight in the Service Industry. While most capital flight involves manufacturing firms, modern technologies now permit firms to export service jobs as well. Carla Freeman examines the information-processing industry in Barbados: "From academic texts to airline tickets, consumer warranty cards, pornographic novels, phone books, specialized scientific articles and literary classics—all have become part of the international high tech information and word processing arena.... On the data entry floor, over one hundred women sit in clustered computer stations, entering data from over 300,000 ticket stubs generated by the 2,000 daily flights of a United States-based airline. One floor below, an equal number of women [enter] data from medical claims [for] one of the largest insurance companies in the United States.... [Companies relocating to Barbados] are entitled to a tax-free period for up to 10 years.... One U.S.-based company that pays $9.50 to its employees within the U.S. pays Bajan employees $2.50 per hour.... The women are heavily monitored by supervisors and the actual computer systems. Computers monitor workers' error rates, speed, quantity of items processed, lapses in keying, and length and frequency of breaks. All are noted and used in measuring productivity and evaluating employees."—Carla Freeman, "From Tourism to Typing: Barbadian Women in the Global Network."[10]

As a result of these changes in technology and policy, many U.S. businesses began to transfer work overseas. Most of the jobs that were lost were in manufacturing: in 1973, manufacturing accounted for 27.3 percent of the non-farm workforce, but by 1990 that share had fallen 10 percentage points.[13] Many companies moved just across the U.S.-Mexico border, where over

2,000 assembly plants, known as *maquiladoras*, were established between 1965 and 1970. Workers in these plants earn less than $1.50 per day, few are unionized, and health and safety regulations are seldom enforced. Many of the workers are women, an increasing number of them single parents, all desperate for work in a country that is in the grip of an economic crisis even more severe than that in the United States.[14] U.S. capital has also "flown" to Southeast Asia, the Caribbean, and Ireland, among other countries.

Back in the United States, workers who had once expected their jobs to last them a lifetime faced a choice of early retirement, often without a pension, or finding a job in the service sector. Steelworkers—both men and women—whose fathers and grandfathers had labored in the mills now turned to jobs at Sears and McDonald's. Service jobs on average pay only 72 percent as much as manufacturing jobs (in 1989), and seldom offer health insurance, pension benefits, or union membership.[15]

Deindustrialization in Action. "Let's look at one company, American Home Products, a New York-based health-care conglomerate that had sales of nearly $7 billion in 1990.... In October 1990 American Home Products announced that within one year it intended to close [a] plant in Elkhart [Indiana] and transfer some of the work to its new plant in Puerto Rico. Among the products to be manufactured in Puerto Rico: Anacin, Dristan, Denorex, and Advil. The move exacted a heavy toll on the Elkhart work force, whose average length of service was fifteen years. More than half of the production workers were women. A survey showed that after one year, of 100 employees laid off, only about half had found other work. In many cases they were forced to accept part-time employment. Their average pay was $6 an hour. Before, it had been $13.40 [and] they had good benefits, including company-paid health insurance. By one estimate, 70 percent of the Elkhart workers lost their medical insurance when the plant closed in November 1990."—Donald Bartlett and James B. Steele, *America: What Went Wrong?*[16]

Union-Busting

Capital flight also affected workers who kept their jobs, as they became far less likely to demand increases in wages or benefits, or to rock the boat by demanding better working conditions or organizing unions. The percentage of workers represented by unions, which had been falling gradually since 1955, now fell sharply.[17] Many unions were forced to sign "concessionary" contracts when management offered them the choice between massive layoffs and cuts in their wages and benefits.

The 1980s also saw a dramatic increase in union-busting activities by employers, beginning in 1981, when President Ronald Reagan fired striking air traffic controllers, members of the Professional Air Traffic Controllers Organization (PATCO). The controllers worked under such stressful conditions that even though they began the job in top physical condition, nearly 90 percent were medically disqualified before they reached retirement age.[18] The strikers were demanding reduced hours, increased decision-making power on the job, and increased benefits and wages. Reagan refused to bargain with the union, fired the workers, had their leaders arrested, imposed heavy fines on the union, and seized its strike fund.[19] Over 10,000 PATCO members were replaced by new trainees, supervisors, and military controllers.

From then on, things only got worse for unionized workers. Employers hired high-priced consultants to help them fight union organizing drives. Using sophisticated advertising campaigns and playing on fears and divisions among the workers, employers falsely claimed that unions would threaten workers' jobs, diminish their freedom, and limit their upward mobility on the job. They also used old-fashioned intimidation, firing those who attempted to organize—even though such firings are illegal and employers found guilty of this tactic are typically ordered to reinstate the workers and award them back pay.

Union-Busting in Action. "An employer can defeat a union campaign and save money, even if the Federal regulators ultimately rule that the employer improperly discharged workers for union activity and order payments of fines and back pay.... Two years ago, the Communication Workers of America tried to organize the workers at the Zurbregg Hospitals ... outside Philadelphia. Larry Cohen, the union's organizing director, said that during the campaign the workers' leader, Betty Watson, a housekeeper in one of the hospitals, was dismissed. A year later, in a hearing before the labor relations board, the hospitals' lawyer admitted that Ms. Watson was dismissed for her union activity, Mr. Cohen said. The hospital agreed to give Ms. Watson back her job, along with back pay. But the loss for a year of Ms. Watson's leadership, along with the fear instilled by her dismissal, broke the back of the recruitment campaign, Mr. Cohen said. A vote of the hospitals' 600 employees on whether to affiliate with the union ended in a tie. A second vote ended in defeat for the union."—Alan Finder, "More Employers Seen Using Dismissals to Fight Unions."[20]

Harvard economists Richard Freeman and James Medoff studied the use of this tactic during the 1970s and 1980s:

> More employers were judged guilty of firing workers for union activity in 1980 [the latest data they had] than ever before. To obtain an indication of the risk faced by workers desiring a union, one may divide the number of persons fired for union activity in 1980 by the number of persons who voted for a union in elections. The result is remarkable: one in twenty workers who favored the union got fired.[21]

As a result of these tactics, union victories were fewer and further between. At the beginning of the 1980s, 23.2 percent of the workforce was unionized; by 1991, organized labor's share had fallen to 16.1 percent.[22]

In many cases, capital flight and union-busting were interrelated strategies: companies fled more heavily unionized states (such as Ohio and Michigan) for states that have so-called "right to work" laws. These laws allow workers at unionized workplaces to forego joining the union—they don't have to pay union dues or support the union in any of its activities, but they still receive all the benefits of the union contract, including union pay scales, health and safety protections, and benefit packages. Twenty states have right to work laws, most of them in the South and West, and in these states unions are much weaker and have fewer members.

Restructuring the Workforce

In addition to moving South or overseas, many companies were able to cut costs in other ways. The most important was by replacing full-time employees with part-timers. Part-timers are not only paid less, but they seldom get fringe benefits such as health insurance and pensions. According to researcher Chris Tilly, "*involuntary* part-time workers—part-time workers who would prefer full-time hours—account for almost all of the growth in the part-time share of total U.S. employment since 1970."[23] Up until 1970, most part-timers were students, parents of young children, or retirees who chose to work shorter hours. Since then, however, employer cost-cutting measures have led to the rapid growth of involuntary part-time work: in 1990, for instance, nearly 5 million workers were involuntarily employed part time.[24] Sociologist Joan Smith reports that

> part-time workers constitute a steadily increasing portion of the labor force and are frequently found in firms open twenty-four hours a day; an increasing number of workers float in and out of jobs depending on seasonal demands. The irony is that the increase in such employment practices signals a vastly increased dependence on a wage labor force that, paradoxically, must be treated in all other respects as though it was entirely dispensable.[25]

The average part-time worker earns only 60 percent as much as the average full-time worker on an hourly basis. Less than 25 percent of part-timers have employer-provided health insurance—compared to nearly 80 percent of full-time workers. Only 26 percent have pension coverage, compared to 60 percent of full-timers.[26] In fact, no matter what the benefit—paid sick leave, paid holidays and vacation, life insurance, or dental insurance—part-timers are short-changed. And, as we will see in the next chapter, women make up more than two-thirds of part-time workers and over half of involuntary part-timers.

Employers have also cut costs by increasing their use of temporary or contract workers. According to economists Heidi Hartmann and Polly Callaghan of the Institute for Women's Policy Research, since 1982 temporary employment through "temp agencies" has grown three times faster than overall employment. Two out of three temporary workers hired through temp agencies are women.[27] Labor reporter Camille Colatosti describes how

> temps now work as computer analysts, lab technicians, customer service representatives, nurses, engineers, and architects. Temps have also entered traditional blue-collar jobs in manufacturing and construction. Almost half of all U.S. hospitals use temps daily. In fact, the health-care industry alone supports 3,000 different temp agencies.[28]

Her research found that clerical temporary workers average $5.11 an hour, without benefits, while manufacturing temps earn between $4.25 (the minimum wage) and $5.25 an hour. A few temp agencies offer health insurance to long-time workers, but the requirements are so strict that few workers ever make it.

If we add together part-time, temporary, and contract workers, the combined category of "contingent" workers includes millions of people: according to one estimate, contingent workers make up between 25 and 30 percent of the civilian labor force.[29] They are most likely to be found in wholesale and retail trade and services, rather than in manufacturing. At Sears, Roebuck, for instance, more than half the workforce is part-time, and other retailers, such as Wal-Mart, are not far behind.[30] None of these contingent workers receive equal protection under government laws, including occupational safety and health regulations, and unemployment insurance and pension regulations. Few are represented by labor unions.[31]

Employers have also turned to homework—sending work out to be done in workers' homes—in order to cut costs. In 1949, Congress passed a law that made industrial homework illegal since it was so difficult to enforce labor standards such as the minimum wage in homework. The Reagan administration re-legalized it and as a result clerical and industrial homework grew during the 1980s. As historian Eileen Boris points out, home-based work can take many forms: traditional garment workers, the new clerical homeworkers, small business entrepreneurs, and independent contractors, all working in their homes.[32]

Homework is typically undertaken to cut costs, not to provide a public service to women. Moreover, as Boris also points out, "Homework deregulation [such as that undertaken by the Reagan administration] addresses not the dilemma of balancing home and family but the desire of some capitalists to weaken both trade unionism and state control over private business enterprise."[33]

One final way of cutting costs has been to hire new immigrants. During the 1980s, immigrants from Latin America and the Caribbean came to the United States seeking work and freedom from political repression. Civil wars, intensified by the Reagan administration's support of repressive dictatorships abroad, led many to seek asylum in the United States.[34] Between 1981 and 1989, nearly 2.5 million immigrants from Latin America and the Caribbean entered the United States legally. Many more immigrated without papers and are known as undocumented workers. It is estimated that there are between 6 and 12 million undocumented workers in the United States, most of them from Mexico, and approximately half of them residing in California.[35] According to the National Council of La Raza, a Latino research and advocacy organization:

> Considerable employment discrimination has resulted from the implementation of employer sanctions provisions of the Immigration Reform and Control Act of 1986 (IRCA). IRCA imposes civil and criminal penalties on employers who knowingly hire or continue to employ individuals who are not legally authorized to work in the United States. According to a 1990 study by the General Accounting Office (GAO), ... an estimated 10% of employers reported discrimination against employees or job applicants solely on the basis of national origin characteristics; an estimated 5 percent had begun a practice of refusing to hire persons based on "foreign" appearance or speech accent ... all in clear violation of the law.[36]

Controlling Labor and Deregulating the Economy

The PATCO strike was only the beginning of the Reagan administration's attack on working people, an attack that continued under George Bush. For instance, both Reagan and Bush appointed people to the Supreme Court and the National Labor Relations Board (NLRB) who could be relied upon to issue anti-labor rulings in key cases. Under Reagan, the NLRB sided with management far more often than in the past. Each victory for management was a loss for labor, and helped demoralize the labor movement.[37]

Reagan also cut back on the enforcement of occupational health and safety standards, halving the number of inspectors and reducing the budget of the Occupational Safety and Health Administration (OSHA), the agency charged with enforcing rules on worker safety. In 1987, the Chicago-based National Safe Workplace Institute estimated that approximately 6,000 workers died between 1980 and 1985 as a result of lax enforcement and ineffective regulation. According to the institute, the workers who died were disproportionately African American, Latino, or young, and held high-risk blue-collar jobs.[38]

Justice in Hamlet, North Carolina. "More than 2,000 protesters weaved their way through the sleepy side streets of Hamlet, North Carolina, on May 2 [1992] to draw attention to unsafe working conditions in the wake of the fatal fire at the Imperial Food poultry plant last September. Twenty-five people were killed and 56 were injured when they were trapped inside the plant by locked fire escapes. The plant had never been inspected during the eleven years it was in operation. Nearly half of the marchers came from out of state.... Workers from farms, catfish plants, hospitals, and factories took their turns at the podium. Each emphasized the theme of the march—'Organize the South! Never Again!'... Imperial Food workers who survived the fire told marchers that the public must never forget what happened at the plant. 'I was left here on the Earth as a testimony to what went on behind those closed doors,' said Ada Blanchard, who escaped the flames. Organizers of the march are demanding the prosecution of Emmett Roe, the owner of Imperial Foods, and a federal bailout for Hamlet workers instead of for the savings and loan industry.... Five days after the march, voters ousted state

> **Labor Commissioner John Brooks, who has been widely criticized for his failure to inspect workplaces. Brooks was defeated by Harry Payne, a state Senator who advocates tougher enforcement of worker safety laws."—Lane Windham, "Marchers Demand Justice in Hamlet."[39]**

Affirmative action programs also became the target of the Reagan and Bush administration's policies. Working together, the executive and judicial branches attempted to turn back the clock on civil rights for racial-ethnic minorities and for women. According to one scholar, starting with Reagan, the government "staffed enforcement agencies with opponents of the legislation, and consistently encouraged legal challenges to past civil rights gains. Reagan's appointees to the Supreme Court were uniformly opponents of the rights of blacks, women and the working class."[40]

Also high on the business agenda was a freeze in the minimum wage. Before 1981 the minimum wage had been increased by Congress periodically in order to maintain low-wage workers' purchasing power at approximately 50 percent of the average manufacturing wage. Starting in 1981, however, the Reagan administration made it clear that it would veto any attempt to raise the minimum wage and Congress lacked sufficient votes to override the veto. As a result, the purchasing power of minimum-wage workers fell by nearly 40 percent during the 1980s.

One striking example of the effectiveness of all these efforts is provided by a Census Bureau study of wages between 1974 and 1990. According to the research, the share of year-round, full-time workers earning wages under the poverty level (for a family of four) rose from 12 percent to 18 percent in these years. High-ranking officials at the Census Bureau attempted to bury the study by taking the unusual step of not issuing any press release at the time of publication, but Maggie Mahar, a reporter for the business weekly *Barron's*, wrote an article detailing the findings.[41]

Undermining OSHA, dismantling affirmative action, and freezing the minimum wage were parts of the deregulation agenda that were specifically aimed at labor. But business also wanted to end environmental protection and consumer safety laws, which they viewed as too expensive. For instance, the Reagan and Bush administrations persuaded Congress to slow down the timetables for improving gas mileage, for reducing polluting automobile emissions, and for cleaning up waterways and toxic waste sites. The share of the federal budget devoted to the Environmental Protection Agency decreased by half between 1980 and 1987. Spending on energy conservation dropped 70 percent during the same time period.[42]

GOVERNMENT BY, FOR, AND OF THE CORPORATIONS

As part of their effort to restructure their operations and bolster their profits, U.S. corporations backed political candidates and parties that would further their agenda. The Reagan administration responded with policies that were aimed at reducing inflation, lowering wages and other business costs, and channeling income from poor and middle-income families to the rich. Freed from what the administration called "burdensome government regulation," and helped by lower tax rates, businesses were expected to start an orgy of production that would bring new prosperity to the country.

This did not happen, as we see in the chapters that follow. At the economic level, Reaganomics failed to follow through on its promises. At a political level, however, it succeeded. In fact, it is now clear that what has come to be called Reaganomics—the Reagan administration's economic policies—was carefully crafted to create a large political constituency that would enable the administration to put in place a program to restore U.S. businesses to health. By promising economic growth and an end to inflation without any economic pain, the Reagan campaign drew millions of formerly Democratic members of the working class—mostly white men—into the Republican camp for the first time since the 1930s, when the Democratic coalition of labor and minorities was cemented under Franklin D. Roosevelt.[43]

The Republicans also used racist and sexist appeals to white male workers in order to woo them away from the Democratic Party. Claiming that women and racial-ethnic minorities were responsible for their pain, the Republicans found a convenient scapegoat for a crisis they had helped to create. Even though the promised gains for workers failed to materialize, the Republicans continued their cheerleading for conservative economic policies and used race and gender imagery to divert workers' attention from the real problems. George Bush, for example, stirred white voters' fears of black criminals through commercials pointing out that his opponent in the 1988 campaign, Michael Dukakis, had granted a furlough to a convicted black rapist, Willie Horton. In 1990, Republican Senator Jesse Helms of North Carolina fought off a challenge from Democrat Harvey Gantt, an African American, with ads that played on racial divisions. The most graphic of these ads portrayed the hands of a white job applicant crumpling up a rejection letter, with a voice-over saying, "You needed that job. And you were the best qualified. But they had to give it to a minority because of a racial quota. Is that really fair?" Of course, the ads didn't mention the high rate of job loss as a result of capital flight from North Carolina to the third world.[44]

Once the Republicans had captured the White House, they put into place a set of policies aimed at restoring business profits. These included controlling labor and deregulating the economy, fighting inflation with tight money, changing federal priorities, and lowering the tax burden on the wealthy.

Fighting Inflation with Tight Money

The Reagan program claimed that it would cut inflation, boost economic growth, balance the federal budget, and bring back "morning in America." Instead, the policies that were implemented plunged the country into a long nightmare of unemployment, debt, foreclosures, and a widening gap between the rich and everyone else.

Earlier, in the late 1970s, inflation had reached double-digit levels. Inflation hurts all those whose incomes do not rise as rapidly as prices. However, some groups have more opportunities than others to protect themselves from the effects of inflation. For instance, retirees on fixed pensions can be badly hurt by rising prices, but in 1972 the government linked Social Security benefits to the cost of living so that benefits rose whenever prices rose. In addition, unionized workers whose contracts include an automatic cost-of-living adjustment were also relatively sheltered from inflation. However, bankers who lend money, particularly for long periods of time, lose during inflationary periods because borrowers pay back with dollars worth less than the dollars they borrowed.

In the late 1970s, the banking sector pressured the Carter administration to rein in inflation. President Carter appointed banker Paul Volcker, a well-known inflation foe, to be the head of the Federal Reserve Board (the Fed, as it is commonly known), the agency charged by Congress with controlling the supply of money and credit. During the early years of the Reagan administration, the Fed had a "tight money" policy, raising interest rates in order to fight inflation. High interest rates can set off a chain reaction that eventually results, as it did in 1981, in a recession: When interest rates rise, people are less able to afford car loans and mortgages, or make the other purchases they usually make on credit. Auto sales fall, construction grinds to a halt, and autoworkers and construction workers lose their jobs. As the chain reaction continues, these workers buy less and still other workers are laid off. As a result of Fed action, then, between

1981 and 1983 the U.S. economy entered the most severe recession since the 1930s. This reduced the rate of inflation from 13.5 percent in 1980 to 3.2 percent in 1982, but it was a disaster for workers. As inflation fell, the unemployment rate soared, averaging 9.7 percent in 1982. Unemployed workers spent less, and retailers were left with unsold products. Goods piled up until businesses were forced to lower their prices to clear out inventories. At the same time, unemployed workers lowered their wage demands in the hopes of finding jobs, and employed workers lowered their demands for wage increases in order to keep their jobs. Lower labor costs meant that companies could hold the line on prices and still expand profits.

Changing Federal Priorities

One goal of this conservative plan was to shift government priorities from social spending to military spending. The Reagan and Bush administrations were determined to restore U.S. dominance by rebuilding the military and asserting U.S. power in all corners of the globe. In Panama, Grenada, and Iraq, hundreds of thousands of civilian and military personnel died as a result of U.S. invasions. In this country, countless others were victims of a shift in priorities that transferred billions of dollars from the civilian to the military budget. In the same period that welfare and unemployment programs for the poor fell by 21 percent, military spending rose by 10 percent (after adjusting for inflation).[45] Increased defense spending was very profitable for companies that supplied the military, who were rescued from the decline in profitability that plagued other U.S. capitalists.[46]

Another important component of the Reagan-Bush plan was to reduce funding for government safety net programs such as unemployment insurance, welfare, public housing, and food stamps. These cuts were made as a way to reduce the size of government and diminish the need for tax revenues. By 1990, only 37 percent of the unemployed were receiving unemploy-

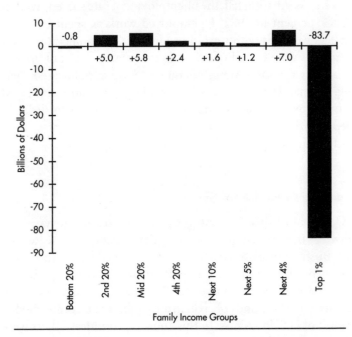

Figure 2-3

Changes in Tax Payments Since 1977
(in billions of dollars)

ment benefits, contrasted with over 50 percent in 1970.[47] As a result of changes in federal and state law, it became more difficult to collect benefits during the 1980s. Benefit levels were frozen or reduced, the duration of benefits was cut, and eligibility requirements were tightened.[48] Similarly, by 1990, the average monthly benefit in the Aid to Families with Dependent Children (AFDC) program—the largest cash benefit program for poor families— could buy 40 percent less than the monthly benefit in the mid-1970s. In this case, Congress and state legislatures had not increased benefits enough to keep up with inflation.

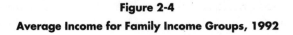

Figure 2-4

Average Income for Family Income Groups, 1992

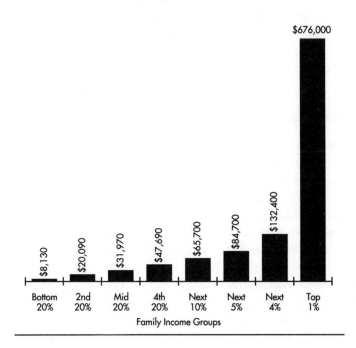

For workers struggling to make it from paycheck to paycheck, Reagan's promise to cut taxes seemed like a dream come true. But in fact the tax cuts that Congress passed in 1981 were sharply tilted toward the rich. Now, more than a decade later, the results are in: during the 1980s, wealthy households saw the percentage of income they paid out in federal taxes drop dramatically, while the tax bite stayed the same or rose for nearly everyone else (see Figures 2-3 and 2-4).

Other changes in the tax code were designed to help corporations rather than wealthy individuals. One example was the

Accelerated Cost Recovery System (ACRS), which increased the amount of revenues that were not taxed. The rationale was to provide companies with funds to modernize their plant and equipment, but most took the additional income and spent it on acquiring other companies, raising executive salaries, or moving their operations abroad—none of which created new jobs in the United States.[49]

ADDING UP THE TAB

Despite all these efforts on the part of the Reagan and Bush administrations, the 1980s saw a continuing deterioration in investment in plant and equipment, in after-tax profits, and in productivity growth.[50] There was a slight recovery between 1982 and 1987, when unemployment rates fell to the lowest level since the mid-1970s. But corporate and government restructuring had so changed the economic landscape that wages did not increase: for the first time since the 1940s, real hourly wages actually *fell* during a recovery![51] All levels of indebtedness—corporate, household, and government—remained at historically high levels. The gap between rich and poor became front-page news across the country. By the late 1980s, the economy had slipped back into recession. Unemployment climbed again, mass layoffs became common, bankruptcies and foreclosures soared. This new recession hit particularly hard, coming on the heels of a recovery that had done little for working people.

All of the economic events and policy responses described in this chapter affected women in their roles as workers in the labor market and in the home. The three chapters that follow examine in detail how different groups of women were affected by the economic crisis and by the conservative policies promoted by business and government. They also look at women's responses to the crisis, highlighting important organizing strategies that women have developed as they fought to protect their rights and their resources.

3

SHORTCHANGED: RESTRUCTURING WOMEN'S WORK

In the previous chapter we saw how, over the past twenty years, corporate and government responses to the economic crisis have led to high unemployment rates, lower wages and benefits, poorer working conditions, and diminished bargaining power for the working class. But the crisis has had different effects on men and women. In some ways, and for some women, the economic crisis has not been as severe as it has been for men. In other ways, and for other women, the crisis has been far more severe.

Throughout the crisis women continued to join the labor force, both to support themselves and their families and to find satisfaction in working outside the home. Companies, seeking to bolster their profits, hired women in order to cut labor costs. In fact, hiring women was a central part of the corporate strategy to restore profitability because women were not only cheaper than men, but were also less likely to be organized into unions and more willing to accept temporary work and no benefits. Women were hired rather than men in a variety of industries and occupations, in the United States and abroad. This led to what has been called the "feminization" of the labor force, as women moved into jobs that had previously been held only by men and as jobs that were already predominantly female became even more so. Economist Jane Humphries has called this process "substitution": "Recession opens up new opportunities for women workers as employers, pressed to cut costs and increase the flexibility of production, substitute women for men within their workforces." Humphries believes that the U.S. economy is now undergoing "a permanent and irreversible mobilization of female labor into the wage economy, and an increasing dependence of both two adult and single adult families on women's earnings."[1] This "feminization" of the workforce, in which women substitute for men, explains why women's unemployment rates, on average, were lower than men's during the 1980s.

Each of the corporate and government responses to the crisis outlined in Chapter 2 had its most damaging effects on a particular group (or groups) of workers. Union-busting, for instance, took its toll *primarily* on the manufacturing jobs that have been dominated by white men (although a weakened labor movement damages the bargaining power of all workers, as we see below). Capital flight also *primarily* affected men's manufacturing jobs, although it also affected women in the service sector and women who work in primarily female manufacturing jobs, such as the garment industry.

SEGREGATION AND SEGMENTATION

The way women experience the economic crisis depends on where they are located in the occupational hierarchy. One concept that will help us understand this hierarchy is *occupational segregation,* which can be by gender—most jobs are held by either men *or* women and few are truly integrated. To take one extreme example, in 1990, 82 percent of architects were male; 95 percent of typists were female. Occupational segregation can also be by race-ethnicity, although this is sometimes more difficult to detect—since racial-ethnic workers are a minority, they rarely dominate a job category numerically, although they may be in the majority at a particular workplace or in a geographical region. At the national level, we have to look for evidence of occupational segregation by race-ethnicity by examining whether a particular group is over- or underrepresented relative to its percent of the total workforce. For instance, if African American women make up 5.1 percent of the total workforce, they are underrepresented in an occupation if they hold less than 5.1 percent of the jobs.[2] Law would be such an occupation: African American women made up only 1.8 percent of all lawyers in 1990. In contrast, they are overrepresented in licensed practical nursing, where they hold 16.9 percent of the jobs.

A second concept that will be helpful in our examination of women's situation during the economic crisis is *labor market segmentation,* a term that refers to the division of jobs into categories with distinct working conditions. Economists generally distinguish two such categories, which they call the *primary* and *secondary* sectors. The first includes high-wage jobs that provide good benefits, job security, and opportunities for advancement. The upper level of this sector includes elite jobs that require long years of training and certification and offer autonomy on the job and a chance to advance up the corporate ladder. Access to upper level jobs is by way of family connections, wealth, talent, education, and government programs (like the GI bill, which guaranteed higher education to veterans returning from World War II). The lower level includes those manufacturing jobs that offer relatively high wages and job security (as a result of unionization), but do not require advanced training or degrees. The fact that unionized workers are part of this lower level is the result of the capital-labor accord described in Chapter 2, through which employers offered some unionized workers better pay and working conditions in exchange for labor peace. In both levels of the primary sector, job turnover is relatively low because it is more difficult for employers to replace these workers. Both the upper and lower levels of the primary sector were for many years the preserve of white men, with women (mostly white women) confined to small niches, such as schoolteaching and nursing.

The secondary sector includes low-wage jobs with few fringe benefits and little opportunity for advancement. Here too, there is a predominantly white-collar upper level (which includes sales and clerical workers), where working conditions, pay, and benefits are better than in the blue-collar lower level (private household, laborer, and most service jobs). Turnover is high in both levels of this sector because these workers have relatively few marketable skills and are easily replaced. For decades, the majority of women of all racial-ethnic groups, along with most men of color, were found in the secondary sector. Mobility between the primary and secondary sectors is limited: no career ladder connects jobs in the secondary sector to jobs in the primary sector.

While most jobs fall into these two sectors (see Table 3-1, which lists the major occupations in each sector), during the economic crisis a third sector began to grow rapidly. This is known as the *informal sector,* or the underground economy. This name is not entirely accurate, however, since these activities do not make up a separate, distinct *economy* but are linked in many ways to the formal, above-ground sectors. Journalist and economist Philip Mattera believes that economic activity can be lined up along a continuum of formality and regulation.[3] At one end there is formal, regulated, and measured activity, where laws are observed, taxes are paid, inspections are frequent, and the participants report their activities to the relevant government entities. At the other end is work "off

Table 3-1
Labor Market Segments

Upper-level primary
- Managerial and professional speciality occupations, except health assessment and treatment
- Supervisors and proprietors, sales occupations
- Sales representatives, commodities and finance
- Farm operators and managers

Lower-level primary
- Health assessment and treatment
- Technologists and technicians, except health
- Protective service
- Precision production, craft, and repair
- Transportation occupations
- Material moving equipment operators

Upper-level secondary
- Health technologists and technicians
- Other sales
- Administrative support occupations, including clerical
- Machine operators and tenders
- Fabricators, assemblers, inspectors

Lower-level secondary
- Private household occupations
- Service occupations, except protective and household
- Handlers, equipment cleaners, helpers, and laborers
- Farming, foresty, and fishing, except farm operators and managers

the books," where regulations are not enforced, participants do not report their activities, and taxes are evaded. Many economic activities exist somewhere in the middle. As the economic crisis deepens, many large corporations, whose own jobs are in the primary sector, have subcontracted some of their work out to underground firms that hire undocumented workers and escape health and safety, minimum wage, and environmental regulations. For example, in El Paso, Texas, only half of all garment industry workers earn adequate wages in union shops.[4] The other half work in sweatshops that contract work from big-name brands, such as Calvin Klein and Jordache, pay the minimum wage, and sometimes fail to pay anything at all. In 1990, the Labor Department fined one contractor for owing $30,000 in back wages and forced him to pay up. Fortunately for the employees, there is some justice in this world: the International Ladies' Garment Workers Union (ILGWU) then won a contract at his shops. According to Mattera,

> operating a business off the books—i.e., without any state regulation or union involvement—is the logical conclusion of the restructuring process. It represents the ultimate goal of the profit-maximizing entrepreneur: proverbial *free* enterprise.... The type of restructuring that has taken place makes it possible for firms that cannot or do not want to go underground to take advantage of unprotected labor nonetheless.[5]

Another reason for the growth in the informal sector is that worsening wages and conditions in the two formal sectors lead people to seek additional work "off the books" to supplement their shrinking incomes and inadequate welfare or social security benefits. Thus the numbers of people suffering what Mattera calls "the nightmarish working conditions of unregulated capitalism" grow rapidly. Women and men of color, particularly immigrants, are those most likely to be found in the informal sector.

WOMEN ON THE EVE OF THE CRISIS

In 1970, the vast majority of women worked in predominantly female jobs, most of them in the secondary sector. However, *which* female jobs they held depended largely on their racial-ethnic background (see Figure 3-1 for the occupational distribution of women in 1970). Few women of *any* racial-ethnic group held jobs in the upper level of the primary sector. Fewer than 20 percent of white women, 12 percent of African Americans, and

Figure 3-1

Occupational Distribution of Women by Race-Ethnicity, 1970

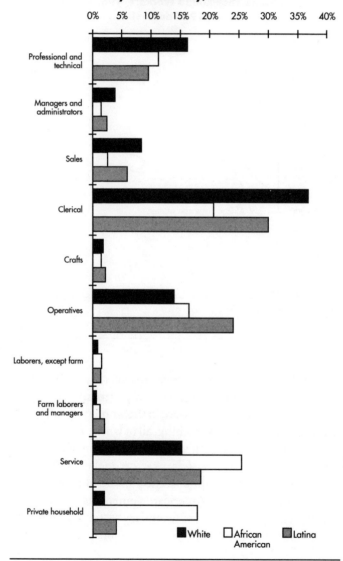

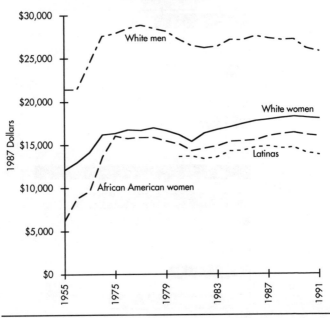

Figure 3-2

**Median Annual Income of Women and White Men,
Full-Time Year-Round Workers, 1955–1991
(in 1987 dollars)**

10 percent of Latinas held either managerial, administrative, professional, or technical jobs. The only primary sector jobs in which women were common were in the women's professions of nursing, library work, and teaching, all of which were dominated by white women who earned much less than white men in primary sector jobs. The secondary sector, on the other hand, was home to the majority of white women and to almost *all* women of color. By 1970, African American women had finally escaped domestic service, a lower level secondary sector job, and moved into manufacturing and other blue-collar jobs, such as sales and

waiting on tables. For Latinas, clerical, manufacturing, and service work were the main occupations, all in the secondary sector.

White women working full-time and year-round earned only 59 percent of what white men earned; African American women and Latinas earned even less, only 50 percent of white men's pay—wage differences that had remained constant for decades (see Figure 3-2).[6] It is not surprising, then, that over 65 percent of families headed by African American women and 30 percent of families headed by white women lived below the official poverty level in 1970.[7] (Data on Latinas were not collected until 1976, at which time over 50 percent of all families maintained by a Latina were living in poverty.)

This situation was bad enough, but many of these indicators of economic distress changed markedly for the worse after 1970 as a result of the economic crisis and conservative policies. The next sections of this chapter examine how women were affected by three of the corporate strategies outlined in Chapter 2—capital flight, union-busting, and restructuring of work—and then look at several of the strategies women used to defend or improve their economic status, including self-employment, moonlighting, and moving into nontraditional jobs. The final section examines the outcome, tracking the gap between women's and men's wages over two decades and examining women's occupational gains to see whether women have in fact penetrated the "locker room" of traditionally male jobs.

The Poverty Line. The poverty line is the level of income that the federal government considers necessary to keep a family out of poverty. In 1992, for instance, the poverty line for a family of four was $13,492. Calculations of the poverty level begin by measuring the annual cost of a market basket of food that contains the minimum nutrients needed to maintain the family in adequate

health. Assuming that the average family spends one-third of its income on food, the poverty line is derived by multiplying the cost of the food budget by three. There are many criticisms of this measurement. For instance, some argue that families spend only one-quarter of their income on food, so the food budget should be multiplied by a factor of four. Others claim that poor families who receive food stamps and other government benefits can actually live below the poverty line and still have an adequate standard of living. Under the current measure, nearly one in seven residents of the United States—over 33 million people—lives below the poverty line.

CAPITAL FLIGHT: A FLIGHT TO WOMEN?

The last chapter described how, over the past twenty years, many U.S. corporations shifted manufacturing jobs overseas. The creation of this "global assembly line" became a crucial component of the corporate strategy to cut costs. In their new locations, these companies hired women workers at minimal wages, both in the third world and in such countries as Ireland. Poorly paid as these jobs were, they were attractive to the thousands of women who were moving from impoverished rural villages into the cities in search of a better life for their families.

But in the United States, millions of workers lost their jobs as the result of capital flight or corporate downsizing. When workers lose their jobs because their plants or businesses close down or move, or their positions or shifts are abolished, it is called worker *displacement*. Over 5 million workers were displaced between 1979 and 1983, and another 4 million between 1985 and 1989.[8] In both periods, women were slightly *less* likely to lose their jobs than men of the same racial-ethnic group. Women in secondary sector factory jobs were hit hardest, primarily because they lacked union protection and the education and skills to find better jobs. (In 1989, over 35 percent of the women in manufacturing operative jobs had less than a high school education.)[9]

Battle in Moore County. "On one side ... is Procter-Silex, a manufacturer of small appliances ... [which] announced plans last spring to shut down two North Carolina plants and ship the 800 jobs off to a *maquiladora* in Juarez, Mexico. On the other side are 800 workers and their families. They are 90 percent women, 50 percent African American and 20 percent Native Americans of the Lumbee tribe. Procter-Silex managers can point to nothing but corporate greed as the reason for this shutdown. They can't blame profitability and productivity, since the plants in question have been among the company's most profitable and are even running three shifts. They can't blame unions and high wages, since the workers are unorganized and get only $7.50 an hour. And they can't blame government regulations, since the state has hardly enforced the few meager protections on the books in this 'right-to-work' state in any case. In fact, twenty or thirty years ago, it was precisely these wide-open conditions that made North Carolina a haven for runaway shops for New England's unionized textile mills. Now the tables are turned.... The shutdown's two year 'social cost' price tag will be $18.87 million, says a study by the Midwest Center for Labor Research. Fortunately, the Procter-Silex workers are not giving up without a fight ... assisted first by the Piedmont Peace Project, a regional group which in turn helped set up a new organization, Moore People's Power. They have waged an intense media and legal campaign aimed at stopping the shutdowns or, at

least, getting a decent severance and retraining package. One particularly effective tactic has been the exposure of the company's toxic dumping. It seems Procter-Silex was not only skipping town, it was planning to leave behind buried dumps of poisonous solvents without any health warning, cleanup, or medical compensation. The workers got environmental groups to denounce the hazards and demand cleanups before any shutdowns took place. They also exposed the hypocrisy of several corporate owners who also sat on the boards of environmental groups."—Federation for Industrial Retention and Renewal News.[10]

The overall result was that even though women lost jobs to capital flight and corporate downsizing, they did so at a slower rate than men. In fact, the share of manufacturing jobs going to women *rose* between 1970 and 1990. Women, in other words, claimed a growing share of a shrinking pie. Sociologist Joan Smith studied this growing tendency to replace male workers with women (as well as a parallel tendency to replace white workers with African Americans and Latinos). In her research on heavy manufacturing industries such as steel and automobiles, Smith found that employers hired men and/or white workers only in those areas of manufacturing where profits were high, jobs were being created, and there was substantial investment in new plant and equipment. In contrast,

> in sectors where profits were slipping, the obvious search for less expensive workers led to the use of Black and women workers as a substitute for white workers and for men.... Close to 70 percent of women in these sectors and well over two-fifths of Blacks held their jobs as either substitutes or replacements for whites or men.[11]

While manufacturing jobs were feminizing, the rapidly expanding service sector was also hiring women in larger and larger

Table 3-2

Employment by Industry, 1970 and 1989

	1970	1989	Percent change
Goods-Producing Industry	**29,543**	**32,918**	**11.4**
Agriculture	3,463	3,199	-7.6
Mining	516	719	39.3
Construction	4,818	7,680	59.4
Manufacturing	20,746	21,320	2.8
Service-Producing Industry	**49,134**	**84,092**	**71.1**
Trans., comm., and other public utils.	5,320	8,094	52.1
Trade	15,008	24,230	61.4
Finance, insur., and real estate	3,945	7,988	102.5
Services	20,385	38,227	87.5
Public administration	4,476	5,553	24.1

numbers—both women entering the labor market for the first time and women displaced from manufacturing. In fact, all the jobs created during the 1980s were in the service sector (see Table 3-2 for a summary of job growth between 1970 and 1989).[12]

A large part of this service sector growth took place in what were already predominantly female jobs, such as nurses' aides, child care workers, or hotel chambermaids (jobs that men would not take), as employers took advantage of the availability of a growing pool of women workers who were excluded from male-dominated jobs.[13] Chris Tilly argues that these sectors were able to grow so rapidly during the 1980s precisely *because* they were able to use low-wage, part-time labor.[14] In other words, if no women workers had been available, the jobs would not have been filled by men; instead, service employment would not have grown as rapidly.

The availability of service sector jobs helped hold the average official unemployment rates for women below those for men. However, the overall figure for women masks important dif-

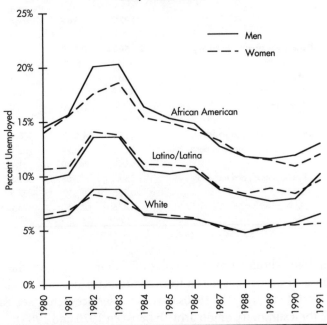

Figure 3-3

Official Unemployment by Race-Ethnicity and Sex, 1980–1991

ferences by race-ethnicity (see Figure 3-3).[15] In addition, the official unemployment rate doesn't tell the whole story. If we construct a measure of *under*employment, we get a different sense of the relative hardships faced by women and men. The underemployed are those who are working part-time but would prefer full-time work, those who are so discouraged that they have given up looking for work, and those who want a job but can't work because home responsibilities—such as caring for children or aged parents—or other reasons keep them out of the labor force. If we look at underemployment rather than unemployment, the rankings change: in contrast to the official

Figure 3-4

Official Unemployment and Real Underemployment Rates by Race-Ethnicity and Sex, 1991

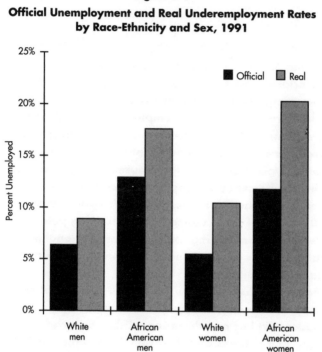

unemployment rates, the underemployment rates are higher for women than for men (see Figure 3-4).

Even though the entire service sector grew during this period, service workers still risked losing their jobs. According to the Census Bureau's study of displaced workers, nearly half of those who lost their jobs between 1981 and 1983, and nearly two-thirds of those between 1985 and 1989, were in the service sector. As the crisis dragged on, in other words, corporate downsizing hit services as well as manufacturing. The financial sector, where women make up 60 percent of the workforce, was particularly hard hit, as jobs in banking, insurance, and real estate were lost as a result of the savings and loan scandal and other financial troubles.

Saving Service Sector Jobs. "Cooperative Home Care Associates (CHCA) is a worker-owned home health care company organized in 1985 and located in the South Bronx. CHCA's 240 employees, most of whom are Latina or African American women from the South Bronx and Harlem, provide health-related and personal hygiene services, light housekeeping, and shopping for homebound people under contracts to hospitals or health service agencies. Approximately 80 percent of these women were receiving public assistance before joining CHCA. Paraprofessional health care workers generally earn less than their counterparts in hospitals or nursing homes, and do not receive medical or dental insurance. In a typical company, these entry-level jobs are at the bottom of a job ladder that has no other rungs. Labor turnover is high, and patients and their families complain about the quality of service they receive. CHCA sets new standards: the average wage at CHCA is $6.50 per hour—high for the industry. The worker-owners have family health insurance and a profit-sharing plan. Twenty CHCA members are earning their nursing degrees through the company. Six people on CHCA's nine-member board of directors are worker-owners, elected by the membership to staggered two-year terms. Florinda DeLeon, a home health care aide and current board member, is involved in all decisions that affect workers. 'I know what this company is about,' she asserted. 'Nothing is hidden. When hard decisions need to be made, you don't feel cheated.'

CHCA actively seeks ways to transfer the lessons it is
learning into the larger industry. In 1987, the company
lent its support to a union-led effort that succeeded in
increasing rates to city home attendant agencies and
tying that increase directly to wages and benefits for
workers."—Sara Gould, "Women Building a Future."[16]

UNION-BUSTING

As we saw in Chapter 2, a second corporate strategy to bolster profitability was to attack labor unions. As the assault took its toll, union membership and union representation declined until by 1990 only 14 percent of women and 22 percent of men were represented by a union—compared to 18 percent of women and 28 percent of men only six years earlier. Even though women are less likely to be represented by unions than men, the *drop* in unionization was not as severe for women, largely because they are concentrated in the service sector where there were some organizing victories. In addition, most women do not hold jobs in factories, the area most vulnerable to union-busting. The drop in unionization was highest among Latinas, who are over-represented in manufacturing, followed closely by African American women. Still, African American women have the highest rate of union representation among women (22 percent) because so many work in the public sector.[17]

The drop in unionized jobs is dangerous for women for several reasons. The most obvious is that unionized women earn an average weekly wage that is 1.3 times that of nonunionized women. The gap is especially large in the service sector, where unionized workers earn 1.8 times as much as nonunionized workers. Figure 3-5 illustrates the union-nonunion wage gap by gender and race-ethnicity.[18]

The loss of unionized jobs also hurts women in nonunion jobs because of what economists call a "spillover" effect from union

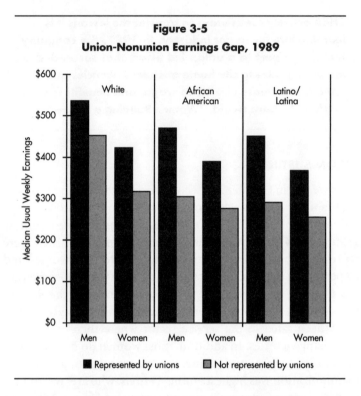

Figure 3-5
Union-Nonunion Earnings Gap, 1989

to nonunion firms in the area of wages and benefits. While it is difficult to estimate the extent of this spillover, Harvard economists Richard Freeman and James Medoff suggest that it raises wages in blue collar jobs in large nonunion firms (those with lower level primary sector jobs) by anywhere from 10 to 20 percent, and also improves benefits and working conditions.[19] This happens for two reasons: (1) nonunion firms must compete for labor with the union firms and therefore have to meet unionized rates, and (2) some firms will keep wages higher than necessary in order to keep unions out. Thus when union workers lose wages and benefits, these spillover effects diminish, lowering wages and benefits in nonunion jobs as well.

Higher wages are only part of what women achieve when there is a strong labor movement. Unionization has an important spillover effect in the political as well as economic arena. For instance, support from the labor movement is responsible for the passage of most of the major safety net legislation in the United States, including the minimum wage and the Social Security Act. When the labor movement is weakened, important items on labor's agenda—including national health care, national child care, improved enforcement of job safety and health regulations, and broadened unemployment insurance coverage—all become more difficult to achieve, even though they address the needs of *all* workers. Further evidence of the critical role played by the labor movement comes from Europe, where family policies (parental leave, child allowances, and national day care) were all enacted with the backing, and sometimes at the initiative, of the labor movement.

WOMEN AND THE RESTRUCTURING OF WORK

As we saw in Chapter 2, a key component of corporate restructuring has involved the use of contingent workers. This has meant that jobs have been transferred from the primary to the secondary sectors, and sometimes even to the informal sector. Economists Eileen Applebaum and Judith Gregory report that employers are increasingly structuring their workforces around a "core and ring" concept.[20] *Core jobs* are relatively secure, have good fringe benefits, and pay salaries that are both high and stable. *Ring jobs,* which are filled by contingent workers, are insecure, have few fringe benefits, and pay wages that are lower than those in the primary sector, even when the work is the same.

Another component of restructuring, and one that particularly affects women, is the use of homework. While homework can provide incomes for women who are unable to locate affordable child care or who live in rural areas, far from other employment, it also exposes women to intense exploitation. Both men and women homeworkers typically earn much less than those who do the same work outside the home: according to the federal Office of Technology Assessment, the poverty risk for homeworkers is nearly double that for other workers. In addition, working conditions in the home can be dangerous. In semiconductor manufacturing homework, for instance, workers are exposed to hazardous substances that can also contaminate residential sewage systems.[21]

Many homeworkers are undocumented immigrants who work out of their homes in order to escape detection by the Immigration and Naturalization Service (INS). During the early 1970s, the majority of undocumented immigrants were male, but since then women have begun to arrive in ever larger numbers:

> Women's migration has traditionally been ignored by researchers.... The INS reported a "dramatic rise" in the number of women apprehended at the U.S.-Mexico border between 1984 and 1986.... Many authors describe a new spirit of "independence" among women choosing to cross the border alone to reunite with family already in the U.S., or to seek employment on their own to support family left behind.22

In the spring of 1990, the Coalition for Immigrant and Refugee Rights and Services in San Francisco surveyed over 400 undocumented women in the Bay Area. Nearly half of them reported employment discrimination by employers who abused them sexually, physically, or emotionally, paid them less than their documented co-workers, or failed to pay them at all. Most of those surveyed worked as domestic servants, in stores, restaurants, and factories.

Homework in Union City, NJ. "Nieves sits in a corner of her Union City kitchen sewing blouses, skirts, pullovers, and bathrobes. Day after day, she hunches over her Merrow machine, lockstitching for 14 to 16 hours at a time.

The clothes she makes are allegedly sold by Seventh
Avenue garment manufacturers to stores like Macy's,
Gimbels, Sears, and J.C. Penney. Resting on the machine,
between her spools of thread, is a picture of Jesus. To
continue living as she has for the eight years she's been
in this country, Nieves says, 'You have to believe in
something.' At age 36, she is doing illegal homework.
She earns $90 to $100 a week, working seven days a
week. Her two children, ages 8 and 11, often help from
the time they come home from school until it's time for
bed. 'They turn collars and cut thread,' she explains....
But even with such low pay, she can't aways count on
money for her work. 'I worked for a fellow who brought
work from West New York and didn't pay when I
finished the work,' she says. 'And when I tried to get it,
he threatened to turn me in to the Immigration. So I
made 100 dozen blouses. They pay $3 a dozen. But I did
the work for free because he never gave me a cent."—
Marilyn Webb, "Sweatshops for One."[23]

WOMEN'S RESPONSES TO RESTRUCTURING

As wages fell and employers pushed more and more work into
the secondary and informal sectors, women responded with a
variety of individual strategies. Some started small businesses.
Others sought "nontraditional" jobs in areas formerly dominated
by men, hoping to earn a man's wage. And a growing number
took on multiple jobs, "moonlighting" in a desperate effort to
make a living wage out of two, or even three, different jobs. Each
of these individual strategies, as we shall see, held some promise,
but all failed to deliver substantial gains except to the lucky few.

SELF-EMPLOYMENT: A CURE-ALL FOR WOMEN?

As the corporate use of contingent workers grew, many women turned to self-employment, starting small businesses of their own. In some of these businesses, working conditions were at the high end of the primary sector: the owners were educated women who were able to use their skills and training in such areas as financial or educational consulting. Others opened small businesses in such low-paid service areas as family day care, tailoring, or catering. The number of women-owned businesses doubled between 1977 and 1987 (the most recent years in which the Census Bureau collected information on business ownership by gender).

But self-employment did not solve women's economic problems. The vast majority of these businesses remained small in scale: although they made up nearly 33 percent of all the businesses in the United States, they earned only 14 percent of the receipts. Nearly 40 percent had total receipts of less than $5,000 a year; only 10 percent had any employees.[24] Even the most successful women entrepreneurs faced difficulties finding affordable health insurance and pension coverage, which they had to buy for themselves out of their profits. Despite conservative rhetoric about the glories of entrepreneurship, self-employment has not proved to be a cure-all for women's economic troubles.

In the third world, self-employment is a far more common strategy among women, particularly as these economies face profound crises. The informal economy is typically far larger than in the United States, and many women have substantial experience as "micro-entrepreneurs." In recent years, grassroots organizations have been able to provide low-interest loans to such women, so that they can avoid borrowing from moneylenders at rates that can run as high as 300 percent a year. Organizations such as SEWA (Self-Employed Women's Association of India) and the Grameen Bank in Bangladesh also empower poor women *collectively* to press for changes in public policy, functioning much like a labor union for self-employed women. For instance, SEWA has worked to change laws that regulate self-employment so that women "micro-entrepreneurs" can achieve higher and more stable earnings.[25]

In the United States, in contrast, self-employment is much more often an individual strategy. Women business owners do not, in general, function as part of a grassroots organizing project for low-income people. In fact, self-employment in the United States often does not empower women, but instead serves the corporate agenda of cost-cutting and union-busting by reducing demands for formal employment in the primary sector. To avoid this problem, women's groups have begun to create organizations, similar to those in the third world, that provide self-employment opportunities to low-income women and organize them as advocates as well as entrepreneurs. These organizations are growing rapidly across the country, although they have as yet only reached a tiny number of women business owners.

Self-Employment for Women. "The experience of the Women's Self-Employment Project (WSEP) in Chicago provides a window on some important dimensions of self-employment. WSEP, a micro-enterprise program established in 1986, runs entrepreneurial training sessions and manages a fund that provides women with small loans [and] targets low-income Latina and African American women in Chicago's inner-city neighborhoods. In the training program, women receive assistance with developing a business plan and applying for loans.... Women demonstrate samples of their products, debate financing and marketing strategies, and organize neighborhood fairs..., learn financial skills and legal regulations which are useful in all aspects of their lives.... Addressing such issues as a group is an empowering process that is difficult to quantify.... If micro-enterprise

programs provide poor women with the means to make informed choices regarding their current and future economic options; if they assist women in developing experience in the area of collective decision-making (as they do when the WSEP circle members decide jointly when and whether a member is ready to borrow); and if they prove effective in developing marketable skills among clients, then self-employment may prove a valuable economic development strategy for moving women toward more active participation in the mainstream economy."—Kavita Ramdas, "Self-Employment for Low-Income Women."[26]

MOONLIGHTING

As the number of poverty-level jobs has increased, more and more women have been forced to turn to moonlighting to boost their incomes. By 1989, 3.5 times as many women were working two or more jobs as in 1973. In contrast, the number of men moonlighting only rose by a factor of 1.2.[27] And many more women were moonlighting because of economic hardship—to meet regular household expenses or pay off debts—not to save for something special, get experience, or help out a family member or friend. African American women and Latinas were the most likely to report that they were moonlighting to meet *regular* household expenses, while white women were more likely to report saving for the future or other reasons—a difference caused by the lower average income of women of color and the greater likelihood that they were raising children on their own.

But moonlighting is ultimately limited by the number of hours in the day. As we will see in Chapter 4, as the crisis wears on and more and more women become fully employed, more families turn to children to help out. According to recent estimates, at least 4 million children under the age of 19 are employed legally, while at least 2 million more work "off the books," and the number is growing.[28] The General Accounting Office estimates that the number of children working illegally has *tripled* since 1983, but even the economist who performed the study believes that his estimates are low because it is so difficult to track illegal child labor. The president of the International Ladies' Garment Workers' Union points out that there are so few inspectors assigned to investigate child labor abuses that it would take *eighty-four years* to inspect all workplaces once. Evidence of serious injury to child workers is mounting: in Massachusetts, for instance, the Department of Public Health found that 28 of every 100 child workers is injured on the job, compared to only 8 out of 100 adult workers. Several hundred child workers are killed each year in the United States.

NEW JOBS FOR WOMEN

During the 1980s, the female labor force grew by over 10 million. Most of the new entrants found traditionally female jobs in secondary sector service and administrative support occupations, since that is where the majority of job growth took place (see Figures 3-6 and 3-7). However, some women made inroads into traditionally male jobs in the highly paid primary sector, and these gains are likely to be maintained. In addition, graduate degrees show how women are increasingly willing to prepare themselves for male-dominated occupations: in 1989, women earned 26 percent of all dentistry degrees, 33 percent of all medical degrees, and 40 percent of all law degrees—compared to 7 percent, 19 percent, and 23 percent, respectively, in 1977. White women were the major beneficiaries of the new opportunities, however, and African American women's share of these degrees in all three areas actually fell.[29] In fact, there has been an occupational "trickle down" effect, as white women improved their occupational status by moving into male-dominated professions such as law and medicine, while African American women

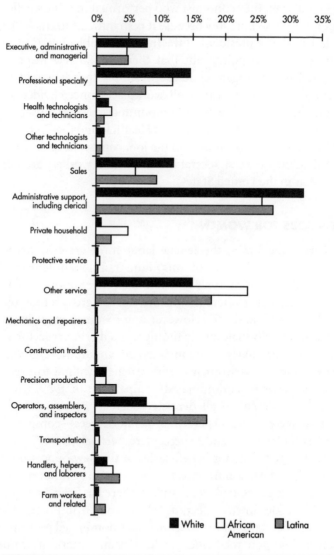

Figure 3-6

**Occupational Distribution of Women
by Race-Ethnicity, 1980**

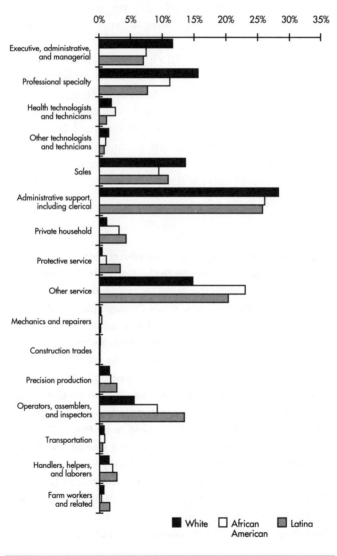

Figure 3-7

**Occupational Distribution of Women
by Race-Ethnicity, 1990**

moved into the *female-dominated* jobs, such as social work and teaching, vacated by white women. There is some evidence that the improvement for white women was related to federal civil rights legislation, particularly the requirement that firms receiving federal contracts comply with affirmative action guidelines.[30]

The movement of women into highly skilled blue-collar work, such as construction and auto-making, was sharply limited by the very slow growth in those jobs. Not coincidentally, male resistance to letting women enter these trades stiffened during the 1980s, when layoffs were common and union jobs were under attack. Moreover, all women lost ground in secondary sector manufacturing jobs, such as machine operators and laborers. Latinas were particularly hard hit, losing ground in most manufacturing jobs.

Hard Times, Hard Hats. "Lisa Narducci gets up at five every morning to commute to the Coney Island Pollution Control Project. With the acrid stench of sewage rising around her, she drills and saws through plywood, crawls over hot concrete, and lifts wooden planks—all part of her day's work as a carpenter. There are no separate changing rooms for her or the other five women on the job. There are no separate bathrooms. The trailers have pin-ups of naked women on the wall. Sometimes, a co-worker or supervisor says he doubts she can do her job. Still, she is glad to be there. Ms. Narducci and other women in the building trades find themselves fighting battles they thought they won years ago. They fight for the few jobs left in the depressed [New York] construction market. They face competitive fears and pejorative comments from their male co-workers. And they are reluctant to complain about working conditions or harassment, believing that troublemakers get dismissed quickly when there are plenty of unemployed replacements. After winning a foothold in the late 1970s and achieving an uneasy peace with male co-workers and bosses in the 1980s, women in the construction industry are seeing their numbers dwindle and their gains disappear.... That is why [Barbara Trees, another carpenter] and Ms. Narducci began a women's committee of carpenters this summer. They want to push to maintain the number of women in the trade and to look for ways to recruit more.—"Hard Times for Women in Construction."[31]

WHAT HAVE THE LAST TWO DECADES DONE FOR WOMEN?

During the 1970s and 1980s, most men earned less as unions declined and as business and government policies took their toll on the male-dominated manufacturing sector. If we use as a measure the median weekly earnings of full-time workers, women in all three racial-ethnic groups improved their standing relative to men of the same racial-ethnic group, and the overall wage gap between men and women narrowed, as did the wage gaps within each racial-ethnic group.[32] But if we compare all three groups of women to *white men,* we see that white women improved the most: in 1990, white women earned 71 percent as much as white men, compared to 63 percent in 1980; African American women only improved from 58 percent to 62 percent and Latinas from 50 percent to 54 percent (see Figure 3-2). This meant that the ratio of African American women's wages to white women's wages actually *fell,* from 92 percent to 88 percent, as did the ratio of Latinas to whites. Opportunities in the labor market, in other words, were not expanding as fast for women of color as they were for whites.

About 40 percent of the overall increase in women's wages relative to men's was the result of the drop in men's earnings.[33] If we break down the data by occupation, we see the same pattern: wherever men's earnings fell, the gap between women and men narrowed.[34]

The picture for fringe benefits mirrored that for wages: the gap between women and men narrowed, partly because men suffered severe losses in benefits. As we saw in Chapter 2, the drive to restructure work included cutting fringe benefits. In 1980, women of all racial-ethnic groups were less likely to be covered under an employer or union-sponsored health insurance plan than men. However, between 1980 and 1987, the share of men covered under such plans dropped more rapidly than the share of women, with Latinos and Latinas once again suffering the greatest losses. Exactly the same pattern held true for pension benefits.[35]

Pay Equity: Union Negotiations Pay Off. "Before her union won pay-equity raises for Minnesota state employees in 1982, Karen Foreman, a clerk typist and divorced parent of two, needed help from the federal government to make ends meet. 'I worked full-time at Moorhead State University, making about $8,600 a year and living in poverty,' said Foreman.... Pay equity, also known as comparable worth, is a remedy for wage discrimination. It requires that workers be paid according to the skills and responsibilities of the jobs they do, not their sex or race. As a result of pay equity, Foreman and other state employees in 150 job categories—mostly women in clerical and health-care jobs—have been brought up to a living wage. Foreman, a ten-year employee, now earns $23,000 annually.... 'It's a matter of dignity,' said Foreman, a member of the American

Federation of State, County and Municipal Employees (AFSCME).... According to 'Bargaining for Pay Equity,' a recent publication of the National Committee for Pay Equity, [a coalition of labor, women's and civil rights groups], 'Since 1979 in the public sector alone, pay-equity adjustments have totaled over $450 million—and unions made it possible.'... 'Unions have done a tremendous amount through collective bargaining to make pay equity a negotiating and organizing issue,' said Claudia E. Wayne, executive director of the pay equity committee [pointing to] 18 pay equity settlements, 12 in the public sector and 6 in private industry."—Carol Kleiman, "Union Negotiations Pay Off in Number of Pay Equity Victories."[36]

Ghettoization and Resegregation

Although the movement of women into male jobs would seem to be good news for women, there wasn't as much integration in these jobs as it would appear. Sociologists Barbara Reskin and Patricia Roos studied twelve selected occupations in which women made gains during the 1970s.[37] They found that in each of the occupations they studied, women specialized in "lower status specialties, in different and less desirable work settings, and in lower paid industries," a process they call *ghettoization.* For instance, even though women moved into the previously all-male occupation of baker, women's baking jobs tended to be inside grocery stores, "baking off" already-prepared baked foods and packaging them. The wages, benefits, and skills of the "retail bakers" were relatively low. In other areas, such as typesetting, women made substantial gains in employment but technological changes in the field meant that the jobs required fewer skills and paid lower wages.

Reskin and Roos also found occupations such as bartending

and retail pharmacy that changed their sex-typing completely, a process they call *resegregation*. Resegregation occurred along racial as well as gender lines: African American women resegregated practical nursing and some relatively low-paid clerical occupations (such as keypunch operator), transforming previously white occupations into ones in which women of color held a disproportionate number of jobs. In virtually all resegregated occupations, wages, benefits, and skills fell, both before and during the switch in sex- or race-typing, so the new entrants failed to realize meaningful economic gains.

Reskin and Roos summarize their findings by pointing to three different reasons for women's inroads into male jobs. In some cases, declining wages and benefits (the result of the corporate strategy to cut costs) made the jobs less attractive to men. In other cases, there was a change in technology, that led to a "deskilling" of the work. Only in a few cases was there genuine integration, and this was generally the result of "pressure from women's groups or regulatory agencies or the dramatic growth that exhausted the supply of qualified men."[38] For instance, women advanced in bank management as a result of litigation. In almost all of the situations Reskin and Roos studied, there was a trickle down effect, as white women moved into men's jobs and women of color moved into female jobs previously barred to them by racism.

Together, these wage and job trends spelled increasing inequality *among* women workers (as well as among men workers). Thus the top 20 percent of earners received 36.7 percent of all women's earnings in 1987, up from 33.4 percent in 1978, while the bottom 60 percent saw their share drop from 43.2 percent to 39.7.[39] Those who were able to establish and maintain positions in the primary sector did very well, but the rest, trapped in secondary and informal jobs, did not.

Up the Down Escalator

If the postwar economic boom had continued into the 1970s and 1980s, women's economic status today would be substantially improved. The crisis produced some gains for women, but many of these evaporate on close inspection. The wage gap narrowed, but partly because men's wages fell. The gap between men's and women's rates of unionization and access to fringe benefits fell, but again partly because men's rates fell. More women entered the workforce, but they also worked longer hours than ever before, held multiple jobs, and sought work in the informal economy in order to maintain their standard of living. Finally, women's gains were not evenly distributed: highly educated women moved even further ahead of their less-educated counterparts.

All this took place against a backdrop of rising family responsibilities. Sociologist Ellen Rosen studied the impact of layoffs, wage cuts, and prolonged unemployment on blue-collar women workers in New England during the early 1980s, a period when textile mills and other factories in the region were declining.[40] She found that the most serious stress faced by the married women she studied was associated with the reduced standard of living their families faced as a result of the cutbacks: "Their continued need to reduce what their wages can buy for their families means that the conflicts they feel between work and family life intensify. Earning less makes it feel harder and harder for them to continue to work and take care of their families."[41]

For these women, who depended on manufacturing jobs, it is not surprising that the economic crisis took a heavy toll. What is surprising is that they experienced it most acutely in the home rather than on the job. Work for them was not a career, a satisfying route to self-actualization, but a fate they accepted in order to provide for their families. When their earnings fell, it was their work at home—the work of marketing, cooking, cleaning, caring—that became more difficult. An increasing number were the sole support of their households. Others found that their household's standard of living could only be maintained if they took on one—or more—paid jobs in addition to their homemaking. They were caught between shrinking incomes and growing responsibilities. The next chapter examines the increasing burden of work in the home during two decades of economic crisis.

4

NEVER DONE: THE CRISIS AT HOME

The household is at once an economic site, where goods and services are produced and consumed, and an affective site, where people come together to meet their needs for intimacy and to nurture the next generation. The past two decades have seen enormous changes in the ways in which households address both their material and affective needs. As we saw in the last chapter, more and more women joined the paid labor force to maintain their households' living standards in the face of a stagnating economy; others entered paid work in search of satisfaction and financial independence. Yet even though women now had fewer hours available for unpaid labor (and for leisure), most continued to perform a wide variety of domestic tasks, including cooking, cleaning, and childcare. Only a privileged elite of employed women, whose jobs put them in the upper level of the primary sector, could purchase these services by hiring housekeepers and nannies.

At the same time, the married-couple family was declining as a percentage of all households, replaced not by any one type of arrangement but by many different types: single-parent families, gay and lesbian families, people living alone, and extended families. The increase in divorce and in out-of-wedlock births meant that more and more children would live with only one parent, typically the mother.

The first part of this chapter describes how women responded to the burdens of unpaid household work during a period of economic crisis. The second section turns to the changes in household composition that occurred over the past two decades, changes that transformed the economic and affective needs of households and the ways that households meet these needs. The final section investigates the consequences of these changes in household composition on women's economic status.

THE HOUSEHOLD AS AN ECONOMIC SITE

Households support themselves by using the proceeds of their paid work to buy goods and services and by putting in hours of unpaid work to care for and maintain their members. This economic function is called *social reproduction*—reproducing the society by maintaining the current generation of workers and raising the next. The term "reproduction" as used here means much more than simply giving birth or providing physical sustenance: children must be socialized to take their place in the economy and in the household of the future; they must be taught appropriate behavior; and so on. In addition, today's workers need to be nurtured and restored from the stress of the workday. Most of the burden of this complex and unquantifiable work of reproduction falls on women, who bear the primary responsibility for childrearing as well as for physically and emotionally sustaining the adults in the household.

Why do women perform so much unpaid work? Why is it that men don't take on an equal share of this burden? Historically, men have been able to command women's unpaid labor through direct intimidation (domestic violence), by excluding women from the paid workforce, by controlling the politics and technology of biological reproduction so that it has been difficult for women to plan childbearing, and by dominating the government so that laws and policies are passed that maintain men's control over women's lives. These efforts not only contributed *directly* to male dominance in the household, but did so indirectly as well, by ensuring that women earned less than men and making them dependent on men for support.

FAMILY SPEEDUP/WOMEN'S SPEEDUP

New research suggests that both in the United States and abroad, the economic crisis has had a double impact on women, affecting both their paid productive activity in the labor force and their unpaid reproductive work in the home.[1] Although the economic crisis has taken different forms in different countries (and even in different regions of the same country), a fall in wages for most of the workforce is common to all economies in crisis. As wages fall, households develop a variety of strategies to protect their standard of living. In the last chapter, we examined one such strategy—the rise of women's labor force participation. A second strategy is to increase the amount of unpaid work in the home.

Such unpaid work is a substitute for wage income. For example, if a woman spends hours cooking and mending, her household will need less cash to buy food or clothing. Thus unpaid domestic work supports business profits indirectly because it means that as long as women are willing to take on the burden of maintaining the household for free, the household can get by with lower wages (which raises business profits). Put another way, if women stopped performing unpaid work in the home today, households would have to hire cooks, housecleaners, laundry workers, childcare workers, chauffeurs, gardeners, and a whole host of others to get the work done. But households could only do this if their wages were substantially higher than they are now. Thus women's work enables employers to pay lower wages than would otherwise be necessary.

Male power in the society at large ensures that it is *women* who perform this work and *women* whose workload rises as a result. In this way, the fact that women are willing to add more and more unpaid labor to their day—at least up to a point—enables employers to reduce wages without lowering the standard of living to a level that would undermine the health and welfare of the labor force. In an economic crisis, the fall in wages bolsters profits, which helps solve the crisis (from the business point of view). This is as true in the third world as in the industrialized countries. According to a recent UNICEF study:

> It would seem, in fact, that poor women represent the principal variable for the policies of adjustment to the present crisis, in the sense that through women it is possible to ensure the survival of at least that third of the population with the lowest incomes, by extracting huge amounts of labor which is not socially recognized.[2]

This is only true in the short run, however, because if household standards of living are threatened by the drop in wages, businesses may face another problem: how to maintain an adequate labor force. For instance, if too many children grow up poorly nourished, the next generation of workers may not produce enough to create profits.

The ability of women to take on more and more work is not limitless. Today's women spend more time in the paid labor force and fewer hours in the home than they did in the early postwar period. They simply do not have enough time for these very time-consuming, cash-saving strategies. In addition, they cannot produce as much in the home as they could in the past. In the 1930s, for example, women responded to falling family incomes by increasing their gardening, canning, sewing, and other activities. Today, many women have lost those skills, live in cities where gardening is impossible, or lack the necessary technology (such as pressure cookers and sewing machines).

THE SECOND SHIFT

As a result of the increase in the number of women in the workforce and the increase in the number of hours worked, more and more women come home to face what sociologist Arlie Hochschild has called the "second shift." The first shift, on the job, is paid; the second shift, in the home, is unpaid. Not surprisingly, this increase in the burden of the double day has left many women exhausted. In interviews with working wives and mothers, Hochschild observed that:

> Many women [could not be torn] away from the topic of sleep. They talked about how much they could "get by on."... They talked about who they knew who needed more or less. Some apologized for how much sleep they needed—"I'm afraid I need eight hours of sleep"—as if eight was "too much."... These women talked about sleep the way a hungry person talks about food.[3]

According to economist Juliet Schor's estimates, women with full-time paid jobs increased their total annual hours of work by approximately 160 hours between 1969 and 1987, an average of an *extra month each year!* Women's hours in the labor market increased by 305 hours, but their household work decreased by only 145 hours. This means that although women's household work decreased, it did not decrease nearly enough to offset the increase in wage work:

> Each additional hour a woman puts into her paid job reduces her household work by nearly half an hour. She spends less time with her children, cooks fewer meals, and does less cleaning.... For both two-earner families and single mothers, the reduction in women's time at home has led to a painful cutback in "household services." Unless husbands are willing and able to pick up the slack, these changes are virtually inevitable: employed women just do not have

the time. Their workloads have already climbed above virtually all other groups.[4]

Men increased the total number of hours they worked by roughly the same amount as women, but for men, 60 percent of the increase was an increase in labor market hours and 40 percent the result of taking on additional work in the household. Although men were doing more housework, including childcare, Hochschild noted two important differences between the jobs typically undertaken by men and women. First, women tend to do more of the *daily* jobs, those that must be done every day on a relatively rigid schedule—shopping, cooking, washing, ironing, childcare. Men take on periodic or occasional jobs, such as washing the car or taking out the garbage, that can be scheduled with more flexibility. Second, women more often take on two tasks at once (cooking *and* childcare), while men concentrate on one task at a time (changing the oil in the car, painting the fence).

Why didn't women's household labor decrease even more rapidly? After all, average family size and number of children both declined during this period. In addition, the percent of women who were married declined, which should have decreased women's domestic labor hours—according to Schor's calculations, the presence of a husband adds approximately 5 hours of housework a week to a woman's workload.

One answer is that men refused to take on *enough* additional hours of housework to lighten the burden carried by women significantly. Despite enormous changes in gender relations, the division of labor between men and women in the average heterosexual household remains very unequal. In addition, the strategies adopted by households to cope with the economic crisis increased the burden on women more than on men. Lower wages meant that most women could not purchase leisure and market substitutes for their domestic labor, which they might have done if wages had risen. In contrast, women at the top of the labor market hierarchy and women living in wealthy households did increasingly purchase leisure time, hiring chauffeurs, housekeepers, nannies, and even personal shoppers.

An Undocumented Nanny. "My dream is to buy a little house and live there with my two daughters who live in El Salvador. I would put up a beauty salon, a fashion shop. Just the three of us, my baby, who's six, my oldest daughter, thirteen, and me…. I feel I'm lucky. The things people would do to have a job like this!… For the first time, I'm in a situation where I feel taken care of. It's different from before, when I cleaned houses. I just didn't make enough. Here, I know I have a stable income of $250 a month. [My employer] doesn't take taxes out yet, because I don't have my papers…. The people of this society have all been good to me. The only thing is that I've been made illegal. But they need us, too. They hire us and because we hunger, we work. Maybe, in our countries, we were secretaries, accountants—and here, maids. What I wouldn't do to work in an office with a computer in front of me! That's what I did in El Salvador."—"Nanny: Confession of an 'Illegal' Caregiver."[5]

With more and more women in the workforce, and increasing numbers of single mothers, the lack of childcare became a crucial social question in the 1970s and 1980s. Childcare, which decreases the burden of women's unpaid work (transferring it to other women, who are paid for the activity), became increasingly unaffordable and, for many low-income women, nearly inaccessible. A 1987 survey found that employed mothers living below the poverty line spent a much larger share of their family income (25 percent) on child care than did those earning more (who only paid 6 percent).[6] Poor children under five were far more likely to be cared for in their own homes by relatives than to be enrolled in an organized child care program, because these programs were too expensive. But this was also becoming increasingly difficult as more and more of the relatives went out to work in the labor market. As a result, working mothers had to rely on a range of private arrangements. Most preschoolers were cared for in their own homes, usually by a relative but sometimes by a paid caretaker, or in a caretaker's home. Only 25 percent of preschoolers were in preschools or group care centers. African American women and Latinas were particularly likely to use family members to care for young children. Still, there is mounting evidence that an increasing number of "latch-key" children had no adult care at all after school.

A Worthy Wage for Child Care Workers. According to the Child Care Employee Project (CCEP), in Oakland, California, childcare workers' wages fell 27 percent in real terms between 1977 and 1988 and their turnover rate rose from 17 percent to 41 percent. The average childcare teacher earns less than $6 an hour, and two-thirds have no health benefits. In response to this situation, CCEP launched a five-year nationwide campaign in April 1992 aimed at raising wages and addressing the working conditions faced by childcare workers. On April 9, designated "Worthy Wage Day," 150 groups in 32 states held marches, rallies, and other events. Centers in Wisconsin raised their fees for one day to illustrate how much childcare would cost if the workers were paid an equitable wage, one that reflected their experience and training; in St. Paul, parents wore stickers proclaiming, "My Job Depends on Quality Child Care"; in Massachusetts, plaster casts of children's hands holding fact sheets on wages in the childcare industry were placed in the State House. "Parents are victims of worthless wages as well," said Marcy Whitebook, Executive Director of CCEP, "in terms of what poor-quality childcare does to their children. Funding for childcare has got to come from the government and employers."[7]

CHANGES IN THE HOUSEHOLD AS AN AFFECTIVE SITE

While the economic crisis took its toll on women and men in the workplace, increasing the hours of labor required to maintain and reproduce a household, the composition of the household itself was undergoing dramatic changes. Across all racial-ethnic groups, in cities and in rural areas, in all regions of the country, the kinds of households that people formed became more and more diverse. The Census Bureau defines two forms of households: "family households," in which those living together are related by blood or marriage, and all the others, which are lumped together as "non-family households." During the 1970s and 1980s, non-family households grew far more rapidly than did family households. Among family households, the most rapid increase came in single-parent households (see Figure 4-1). Falling birthrates, rising divorce rates, and fewer marriages meant the Ozzie and Harriet family of the 1950s was no longer the norm.

The new diversity of family forms affected the economic fortunes of women and children, some for the better and some not. The presence or absence of another adult wage-earner, the size of the family, the ages of children, and the degree to which women could count on income from absent fathers or family members—all determined economic status. Some changes associated with the new family forms (such as decreases in average family size) improved women's economic status, but most diminished the financial resources available to women.

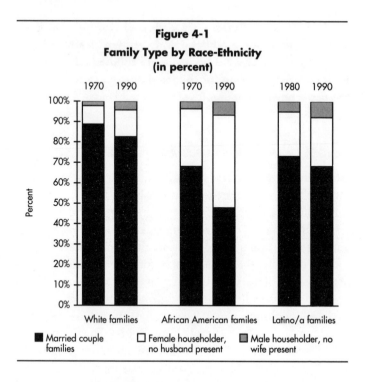

Figure 4-1
Family Type by Race-Ethnicity
(in percent)

White families — African American familes — Latino/a families

■ Married couple families   □ Female householder, no husband present   ▨ Male householder, no wife present

The Rise in Nonmarriage

Perhaps the most important change for women was the increase in the category the Census calls "nonmarriage"—single and divorced women. The percent of women between the ages of 20 and 24 who had never been married rose from 36 percent to over 60 percent from 1970 to 1988 (see Figure 4-2), although there were major differences among racial-ethnic groups: 75 percent of African American women in this age group had never been married, compared to 60 percent of white women and only 50 percent of Latinas.[8] One reason for the rise in the nonmarriage category was that women were getting married later—by 1990 the average age of first marriage had risen from 21 to 24 years of age (the oldest recorded age since the Census Bureau first began

Figure 4-2

**Percent Never-Married 20 to 24 Year Olds, by Sex
and Race-Ethnicity, 1970, 1980, and 1988**

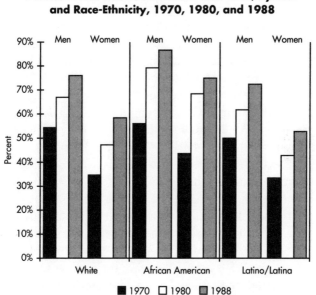

keeping records on marital status). In addition, the divorce rate rose sharply, particularly during the 1970s. In 1985, over 23 percent of ever-married women had been divorced, up from about 14 percent in 1970.[9]

As family living arrangements underwent a dramatic transformation, the number of children per family fell, partly because an increasing share of married couples were childless and partly because many others chose to have smaller families. As married couples had fewer and fewer children, the share of all children who lived with both parents necessarily declined. What conservatives decry as an explosion in out-of-wedlock births is actually more a result of fewer children born to married-couple families than of more children born out of wedlock. As nonmarriage increased, so did single motherhood. In 1970, only slightly over

11 percent of families with children were maintained by women alone (no husband present); by 1988, the figure was nearly 25 percent.

Here again, there are important differences by racial-ethnic group. In 1988, African American women were the sole support of more than 50 percent of all families with children, Latinas of under 35 percent, and whites of under 20 percent.[10] Demographers estimate that 60 percent of the children born in the 1980s will spend some portion of their childhood living with only one parent.[11] In 1990, 14 million children were living with their mothers alone. Of these, 410,000 (just under 3 percent) lived with teenage mothers.[12] Despite media hysteria over an "epidemic" of adolescent pregnancy, the teen birth rate has actually dropped steadily over the past few decades (see Figure 4-3). What is different is that today most teen mothers choose both to keep their babies *and* not to marry, either deferring marriage, choosing women partners, or deciding not to marry at all. In contrast, teen mothers in the 1950s more often gave their babies up for adoption or married the father. In any case, single motherhood is increasing most rapidly among older women so that teen mothers accounted for only 20 percent of single mothers in 1990, compared to 50 percent in the 1970s.[13]

The fall in the average number of children per household is part of a long-range trend that is taking place in all industrialized societies: as children cease to be economic assets, useful for their labor on the farm or in the factory, and become economic costs (for education, for instance), birth rates decrease. This trend has been aided by the rise of private pensions and social security, which take some of the responsibility for supporting the retired generation from their children. Parents no longer need children to support them in their old age. And at the same time as the economic need for children has declined, the cost of raising them has increased, both in time and money. Today's parents, particularly mothers, are held responsible for their children's intellectual, emotional, and physical health, which leads many women

Figure 4-3

Birth Rates by Age of Mother, 1970, 1980, 1988

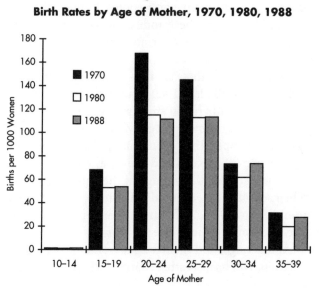

to have fewer children so that they can devote more time and energy to each child. This trend has been accelerated by the stagnation in household incomes and the time squeeze described above.

There was no one cause for all these changes. The so-called "decline in family values," which the conservatives blame for all our social and economic problems, is actually a complex mixture of economic, cultural, and political factors. And while conservatives may see a "breakdown" of the family, others—including many women—argue that women and men are being freed from traditional modes of family life and the choices available to them have broadened. Very similar changes in household composition have taken place in Japan, Canada, and the major Western European nations, during the same period: fertility and marriage rates have declined, and there have been increases in out-of-wedlock births, the average age at first marriage, cohabitation, and divorce rates. Married-couple households declined as a share of all households in all of these industrialized countries except Japan,[14] and this despite the enormous differences in religious, social, and cultural values.

One factor that made these changes possible was the women's movement. During the late 1960s and early 1970s, women all across the country gathered in small groups to talk about common problems. As the movement grew, they began to take action: they established rape crisis centers and shelters for battered women, they marched to demand equal pay and equal access to credit, they worked for the passage of the equal rights amendment. Their activities called attention to the prevalence of domestic violence and rape, the limited occupational choices available to women, the waste of women's education in a traditional marriage, and the need for women to define themselves on their own terms, rather than in terms of a relationship to a man.

Hand in hand with these lessons from the women's movement came a decline in the social stigma of not being married. The term "spinster" was replaced by the more positive "career woman." Unmarried young people left their parents' homes to live alone or with other young people in apartments, a lifestyle that was less common in the 1950s. Changes in the law, beginning in the early 1970s, introduced no-fault divorce, eliminating the need to prove adultery, desertion, or cruelty in order to get a divorce. Once couples could simply declare the marriage "irretrievably broken," rather than make a case that one or the other party was at fault, divorce became easier to obtain and far less costly, financially as well as emotionally.

The gay rights movement, catalyzed by the 1969 Stonewall riots (when patrons of a gay bar in New York City fought back against a police raid), enabled many gays and lesbians to come out of the closet of fear and silence. Urbanization and increased geographic mobility provided gays and lesbians with opportunities to escape the traditional norms of small-town life, and they migrated to cities such as San Francisco in search of the freedom to live openly. There are no systematic or comprehensive data on gay and lesbian households because the Census Bureau does not identify the sexual orientation of those it surveys. However, a study by the Kinsey Institute found that one-third of all lesbians have been married and one-half of these are parents. In addition, an increasing number of lesbians are choosing to bear or adopt children. Some studies suggest that lesbians have a higher labor force participation rate than heterosexual women, are more likely to have higher education, and have annual incomes greater than the U.S. average. However, we do not know the poverty risk for lesbian households, the extent of labor market or housing discrimination they face, or the economic consequences of breakups in lesbian relationships.[15]

Gays and Lesbians Win Right to Benefits. "Although employers are cutting benefits wherever they can, one area in which workers are winning the right to more benefits is the demand for 'domestic partner' benefits by gay and lesbian workers. Gay rights activists point out that nontraditional families are discriminated against since they receive a substantially smaller amount of employer-provided benefits than married-couple families. In addition, marriage brings a variety of other economic benefits such as social security survivor's payments and lower rates for family memberships at health clubs. Eight cities have recently passed ordinances providing some form of health benefits, sick leave and/or bereavement leave for domestic partners of city employees, including Berkeley, Los Angeles, Seattle, and New York City. A number of private companies are reconsidering the meaning of family: for instance, some

> health clubs now offer partner discounts, and five in-
> surance companies now underwrite plans for domestic
> partners. And court decisions in New York and Mas-
> sachusetts during the early 1990s have also begun to af-
> firm the 'family' rights of gays and lesbians."—Patricia
> Horn, "To Love and to Cherish."[16]

Finally, nonmarriage may have increased because of a decline
in male responsibility—a flight from the family. According to
writer Barbara Ehrenreich, beginning in the 1960s men seized
upon the sexual revolution made possible by the widespread use
of the birth control pill to liberate themselves from the responsibilities of a wife and children. Men's magazines glorified the
bachelor life, and men began to marry later and divorce more
frequently, especially to marry younger women.[17]

THE ECONOMICS OF NONMARRIAGE

All these changes in family and household structures took
place in an economic context that favored nonmarriage. For
instance, as male unemployment rose among African Americans,
their marriage rates fell. According to sociologist William Julius
Wilson, in regions where African American male unemployment
rates were highest, marriage rates were lowest. Many of these
regions had been hard hit by corporate capital flight: factories had
left the cities to which African Americans had migrated in the
earlier part of the century, leaving behind high rates of unemployment and underemployment. While many of the women were
absorbed into the service sector, the men were left out in the cold.
And without jobs, they were less likely to marry since it was
expected that men support their wives financially. According to
Wilson, "... unlike white women, black women—and particularly
younger black women—are confronting a shrinking pool of
economically stable, or 'marriageable,' men."[18]

There is evidence that the same capital flight also affected the marriage rates of Puerto Rican men but not those of Chicanos, who were less likely to work in industries that experienced such deindustrialization. In fact, the growth of the informal economy, with its dependence on immigrant labor, may have provided some Chicanos with jobs, even though these were low paid and lacked benefits or job security.[19] Consistent with Wilson's hypothesis, Puerto Ricans are far less likely than Chicanos to live in married-couple families.

Further evidence of the link between economic crisis and marriage rates was found by researchers at the Children's Defense Fund, a Washington-based advocacy and research organization that lobbies for a child-centered public policy. These researchers also found that employment difficulties helped to explain the growing percent of younger men who were unmarried. For instance, in 1973 the typical male high-school dropout found a full-time job at about age 22; today, however, it can take as long as four more years—until age 26—for that dropout to find full-time work, largely because so few jobs are open to workers who do not have a high school degree and because so many firms have restructured jobs from full to part time.[20] The average annual earnings of dropouts were cut in half between 1973 and 1986:

> As a result, many young people are postponing marriage or choosing not to marry as a result of declining earnings rather than brighter career prospects. Regardless of their race or level of educational attainment, young men ages 20 through 24 with earnings above the poverty threshold for a family of three remain three to four times more likely to marry than young adult males with below-poverty earnings.[21]

The rise in nonmarriage among African American women can be traced to two additional factors: the gap in life expectancy between African American men and women and the increasing number of African American men who are in prison. African American women have always outnumbered African American men, partly because occupational hazards have claimed so many of the men's lives. As Johns Hopkins University professor Vicente Navarro has pointed out:

> The working class has much higher rates of mortality than managerial and professional groups. [In 1986], the mortality rate for heart disease was 2.3 times higher for blue-collar workers (operators) than for corporate lawyers or physicians (managers and professionals). These class differentials are much higher than white/black mortality differentials. And the class mortality differentials between, say, blue-collar or service workers and corporate lawyers, physicians and bankers have increased during the 1980s—even more than race differentials. These growing class mortality differentials, ignored by our government and our media, are primarily responsible for the growing mortality differentials between whites and blacks.[22]

The economic crisis not only widened the mortality gap between whites and African Americans, but it also widened the gap between African American women and men: relatively more African American men than women fell victim to homicide, lost health coverage, or died from treatable diseases. Life expectancy for African American men *fell* in the late 1980s. As a result, the number of unmarried African American women continues to exceed the number of men. For instance, in 1990, there were 86 unmarried African American men for every 100 women between the ages of 25 and 29.[23]

In addition, the "war on drugs," with its arsenal of repressive measures, including mandatory sentencing, has led to the incarceration of increasing numbers of men, disproportionately men of color. In 1990, the United States had a larger percent of its population in prison than any other country in the world—more even than South Africa. The number of people incarcerated almost tripled between 1970 and 1990. Nearly 25 percent of African American men between the ages of 20 and 29 are in prison, on probation, or out on parole.[24] (At the same time, there are waiting lists at virtually every drug rehabilitation program in the country.)

These factors have all helped increase the number and percent of African American women who are not married. But women are not merely the passive victims of economic trends that have diminished what Wilson calls the "pool of marriageable men." African American women, like white women, have also increasingly *chosen* to live in households without men—even though the economic consequences of such a choice are more severe for African American women than for white women. (In 1990, the median annual income of women maintaining families on their own was $19,528 for whites, compared to $12,125 for African Americans.)[25]

While African American men may have remained unmarried because of economic constraints, some women were able to make a choice for autonomy, a choice made possible by new labor market opportunities rather than the inability to find a suitable male partner. Thus the only region of the country where the share of women-maintained households rose even though there was a rise in the number of "marriageable" males was the West, where African American women have higher employment rates, higher average incomes, and lower rates of poverty than African American women elsewhere in the country.

As we saw in Chapter 3, the 1970s and 1980s saw increased women's workforce participation, which increased these women's autonomy, making it possible for them to support themselves and their families without a male income—even though their wages were generally so low that they did this at the cost of a very low standard of living. Economist Heidi Hartmann has discussed this seemingly paradoxical result of the economic crisis:

> There is [a] tendency to view capitalist crises as necessarily negative. There can be no question that budget cuts, unemployment, and poverty make people's lives worse and that women are particularly severely affected by them; inasmuch as these are the short-run effects of the current crisis, they are serious and unhappy results. But the longer structural transformation ... has had and will

continue to have many positive effects, particularly for women, inasmuch as it entails fundamental changes in gender relations as well. Placing gender relations at the center of the analysis causes us to have a very different view of the transformation. There is potential now for continued truly revolutionary changes in our intimate lives and in women's ability to be economically autonomous (perhaps for the first time in human history).[26]

Given new opportunities, women left their marriages, delayed them, chose women as their partners, or chose to live (and have children) alone. Through all these changes, however, one thing remained constant: women remained responsible for their children. As a result, women who divorced generally retained custody of their children, either by choice or by necessity, as did women who bore children out of wedlock.

Teen mothers face particular difficulties. Few schools are structured for the teen parent, childcare costs are prohibitive, and schooling often has to be interrupted. However, recent work by Arline Geronimus and Elaine McCrate suggests that teen pregnancy itself may not be as economically harmful as is generally believed. They find that the likelihood of poverty is not increased because teen mothers tend to be poor already: in their view, the poverty faced by teen mothers is as much a *cause* as a consequence of teen motherhood.[27] Researchers at the University of Pennsylvania who followed a group of African American teen single mothers from Baltimore for seventeen years argued:

> The popular belief that early childbearing is an almost certain route to dropping out of school, subsequent unwanted births, and economic dependency is greatly oversimplified, if not seriously distorted. A substantial majority of the young mothers in our study completed high school, found regular employment, and even when they had been on welfare, eventually managed to escape from public assistance. Relatively few ended up with large families.... The women in the Baltimore study, for the most part, displayed a remarkable commitment to their children by juggling school, work, and child-care responsibilities.[28]

Nonetheless, cutbacks in social programs in the late 1980s have made teen motherhood increasingly difficult. Many states have considered punitive changes in welfare eligibility to discourage teen childbearing, and few states provide the supportive services that teens need in order to manage school, mothering, and a job.

A Different View of Teen Mothers. "[Let's consider] two New York mothers with one child each, both daughters named Katherine. One mother, Katherine D. La Guardia, is an accomplished physician and granddaughter of the man many consider the city's greatest mayor. She is married. Her Katherine is 3 years old, and proud to walk rounds with her mother. The other is Yveline Sylvaine, who came from Haiti at 9, became pregnant at 11 1/2 and is unmarried. She won hard battles to keep her child, holds two part-time jobs and, at age 21, is a senior at Hunter College, from which she will graduate a semester early. Her Katherine is 8, and brags about her mother's accomplishments. These two mothers are united in their dedication to young, pregnant, poor women. Dr. La Guardia, 37, addresses their needs as director of the Women's Health Clinic in New York Hospital. Ms. Sylvaine, as part of one of the clinic's programs, volunteers as a mentor to a 17-year-old pregnant woman whose father is in jail and whose mother has AIDS. The two met a year ago when ... the doctor asked Ms. Sylvaine if she would counsel a frightened young mother-to-be, ease her over the rough spots, lend an ear. Why not? Besides mothering, studying, giving out investment information for Citibank during the week and working at a psychiatric center weekends, Ms. Sylvaine had plenty of free time. [Dr. La Guardia] attacks those who consider teen-age pregnancy an epidemic.... She

cites research findings that most teen-age mothers don't
go on to have more than three children, and that twenty
years later, most have jobs [and] she says more teen-
age motherhood is inevitable. And that can be good or
bad. To assume it is bad leads to a cataclysmic con-
clusion. One million babies are conceived by teen-agers
each year. More than half are born."—Douglas Martin,
"Teen-Agers with Children Also Breed Love."[29]

FROM ECONOMIC CRISIS
TO HOUSEHOLD REPRODUCTION CRISIS

These transformations in the family, occurring simultaneously
with (and partly as a result of) the economic crisis, could open
the door to major restructuring of relations between men and
women, particularly if social policy were changed to adapt to the
new realities. For instance, family policies that equalized the
standard of living between one-parent and two-parent families
could reduce the costs that women are forced to pay for their
autonomy. In Sweden, single parents receive a payment from the
government to help them support their children. However, it was
difficult to get progressive social policies enacted in the increasingly conservative and anti-government political environment of
the 1980s. Even a bill that provided unpaid family leave failed to
pass over a presidential veto in 1992.

In this punitive context, which we explore in more detail in the
next chapter, transformations in the family are more likely to
combine with decreases in wages to create a *reproduction* crisis,
in which some households are simply unable to provide for their
most basic economic needs, threatening the health and welfare
of the next generation of workers. Some of the physical conditions that suggest such a reproduction crisis are childhood
hunger, increases in infant mortality, and a rise in stress-related
work disabilities. One indicator of the extent to which the

mechanisms of caring for the next generation have broken down is the increase in the number of children living in foster homes or other institutional settings. Another is the huge increase in homelessness. While the popular stereotype of the homeless is a single man, the fastest growing group of homeless persons is families maintained by a woman. Single-parent families, the vast majority maintained by women, account for at least 75 percent of homeless families.[30]

The term "feminization of poverty" refers to the increasing share of poor families that are headed by women. Researcher Diana Pearce, who first coined the term, pointed out that in 1990, families maintained by women were nearly twice as likely as married-couple families to have income below *half* of the poverty line.[31] Pearce also believes that the official poverty data tend to underestimate the number of women living in poverty since many single mothers will double-up with relatives, such as parents, to save on housing costs. But in this case the Census only counts them as one family, rather than two. Furthermore, the rapidly increasing numbers of women-maintained families among the homeless—people who are missed by the official Census—are not counted.

As economist Nancy Folbre has pointed out, it would be far more accurate to call the "feminization of poverty" the "pauperization of motherhood."[32] In 1959, when the Census Bureau first began calculating the poverty rate, less than 25 percent of all families in poverty were supported by a woman; in 1990, the figure had doubled, to over 50 percent (see Figure 4-4). But this increase occurred almost entirely among women supporting children—in fact, the poverty rate for single women without children fell as their labor force participation grew, as the government established a more adequate safety net for older women, and as women's access to higher-paying jobs increased.

For obvious reasons, single mothers are far more likely than married-couple families or single fathers to live in poverty. Single parents of young children need childcare if they are to join the

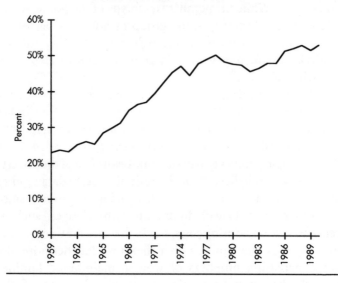

Figure 4-4

**Families with Female Householder as Percent
of All Poor Families, 1959–1990**

labor force, but since women continue to earn less, on average, than men, it is more difficult for single mothers to afford childcare. In 1990, for instance, the median income for single mother families with children was approximately $13,092. This was 32 percent of the average married couple's income and 52 percent of the average single father's income.[33] These were the same women who typically paid 25 percent of their income for childcare.[34]

Inadequate child support payments also contribute to high poverty rates among single mothers. Despite recent changes in the law that have tightened enforcement, the amount of money transferred from men to women is, on average, much less than the actual cost of maintaining the children. In 1987, for instance, the average amount of child support received was $2,710, which made up less than 20 percent of household income.[35] The average payments received by white women were nearly twice as high as those received by African Americans and 12 percent higher than those received by Latinas.

Race and education largely determine whether a woman receives adequate child support: all women with college educations, as well as white women, were far more likely to have been awarded child support by a court than women with less education and women of color. White women and college-educated women were also more likely to have been awarded health insurance benefits. However, having a court order is no guarantee that a woman will receive child support: in 1987, less than 75 percent of those who had been awarded payments by the courts actually received them.

A Deadbeat Dad. "After fifteen years of marriage and six children, Richard Paul Hilliard took a powder. As his ex-wife, Eileen, tells it, he quit his mid-level government job, gave her almost none of his earnings while working as a contractor, and eventually took off with everything of value from the couple's Fairfax County home, including his wife's Ford van. Now, several years later, Hilliard ... is reported to owe nearly $30,000 in child support. 'I haven't the faintest idea' where he is, Eileen Hilliard said in an interview, squeezed in between her full-time job as a management assistant at Fort Belvoir and her night job at a pet store in Franconia.... She repeatedly gave authorities her husband's whereabouts before he took off for good, but they never properly served the court summons on him, she said. As a contractor, he was able to get paid in cash, a common method delinquents use to prevent legal action against paychecks or bank accounts. Hilliard did leave his wife some things:

his outstanding electrical and medical bills and overdue taxes, along with their mortgage payment."—Sandra Evans, "Putting a Face on Deadbeat Dads."[36]

There are a number of reasons for the failure to pay. Some men have remarried and are unable to support both the old and new families, some have lost their jobs, some are enjoying the bachelor life, and some withhold payments as a form of revenge. In addition, until recently child support awards were seldom enforced, and even today most of the effort goes toward finding absent fathers when the mothers are collecting welfare—and then the state keeps most of the money it collects. This is despite a federal law passed in 1984 that gave the states the power to withhold child support payments automatically from an absent father's paycheck (like income taxes). That same law required that the states adopt uniform guidelines for calculating the amount of child support to be awarded to the custodial parent. Some states set the amount at a flat percentage of the absent parent's income; others require both parents to contribute in proportion to their incomes. These new guidelines are apparently leading to higher awards, but child support alone cannot equalize incomes between single-mother and married-couple families.[37] If all women received all the child support they were due, only a quarter of the gap between their income and the poverty threshold would be closed.[38] A far greater portion of the gap would be closed by increasing women's earnings and income support from the government, rather than focusing on the individual father.

The state has been a major contributor to the impoverishment of the single mother. It has repeatedly cut back Aid to Families with Dependent Children (AFDC), the major income support program for poor children, over the past twenty years. Not only do fewer children living in poverty receive AFDC but the purchasing power of the average AFDC check fell by 42 percent between 1970 and 1991.[39]

The Homelessness Crisis

Women's vulnerability to homelessness can be traced directly to their economic and social status. Women earn less than men, can count on little support from the absent father, and have experienced major cutbacks in government assistance. Women who maintain households are therefore far more likely to be renters than homeowners. According to the Women and Housing Task Force of the National Low Income Housing Coalition:

> Between 1975 and 1985, the median rent for private unsubsidized rental units rose 20 percent in real terms. Over the same period, the real median income of renter households with two or more persons maintained by women fell by 12 percent. Not surprisingly, rent burdens among young single-parent households skyrocketed from an average of 38 percent of their incomes in 1974 to 58 percent in 1987.... The supply of low-cost rental housing is disappearing. There are now more than two low-income households for each affordable unit.... Today, although the Department of Housing and Urban Development (HUD) provides subsidies to 4.3 million households, this is only one-third of those in need.[40]

And this situation is not expected to improve: housing will remain in short supply in the coming decade, and homelessness will increase.

In addition, women with children face discrimination in finding housing, which increases the odds that they will not be able to find rental apartments at a reasonable cost. A HUD survey in 1980 found that 25 percent of all landlords barred tenants with children, while another 50 percent had partial restrictions, such as on the age or number of children. As the supply of low-cost units has shrunk over the decade, housing discrimination against children has increased. At the same time, women seeking apartments can face sexual harassment from potential landlords (and that harassment often continues even after they sign a lease).

WRATH. "Two women from Vacaville, California, recently formed WRATH, Women Refusing to Accept Tenant Harassment—the nation's first advocacy group to help women who face situations of sexual harassment from landlords, owners, or managers. Two dozen women in the Fairfield North complex complained about [a] manager ... who had keys to all apartments—which he used at any time of day or night. The women feared eviction from their affordable public housing if they didn't submit to [his] sexual advances.... Harassed tenants had secret meetings in their apartments and organized to take legal action. Though it took them two years to obtain any legal information on tenant harassment, the women eventually won their civil case against [the manager], which resulted in a $1 million settlement and his termination. When invited, representatives of WRATH will meet with tenants experiencing harassment, provide them information, and explore options for organizing."—April Gertler, "Wrathful Tenants United."[41]

Finally, domestic violence is a major contributor to homelessness. According to one report, *half* of all homeless women and children are fleeing domestic violence. Critical shortages in the availability of transitional and shelter housing exacerbate the risk of homelessness for victims of violence.[42] In 1987, although 375,000 battered women and their children were given emergency shelter, another 150,000 were turned away for lack of room. Most shelters place limits on the time a family can stay, but for all the reasons described above, two weeks, or even three months, is rarely long enough for a woman to find a safe and affordable apartment. Analysts of the housing market predict that homelessness will grow in the coming decade, placing even more women and children at risk.

The families most at risk are those who were living on the margin at the onset of the crisis. Poor African American and Latino households, and particularly households maintained by women of color, risked poverty before the crisis, but now an increasing number of them risk a reproduction crisis. For them, poverty is an indicator of the risk of an even more devastating social breakdown.

Domestic Violence as Public Art. "Feminists have exposed the private secrets of domestic violence by bringing the abuse of women and children into the public spotlight. It should not come as a surprise, then, when a feminist artist who wants to address domestic violence shuns the route of the private art market and turns instead to public art forms.... Peggy Diggs, of Williamstown, Massachusetts, is that sort of artist. Her work ... reveals the horror of abuse while denying the public/private division that protects the 'sanctity' of the home. [One facet of her work] was inspired by a woman prisoner in Rhode Island who told Diggs that her violently abusive husband ... only allowed [her] out of his presence to go grocery shopping, hence her idea for the message to be planted in a grocery store setting for easy access to all women. Tuscan Dairy Farms of Union, New Jersey, agreed to support the project with Creative Time, a group that sponsors artwork in public places. In January and February one and a half million milk cartons were produced and distributed in New Jersey and New York. Next to an image of an aggressively raised hand were the words: WHEN YOU ARGUE AT HOME, DOES IT ALWAYS GET OUT OF HAND? The telephone number for a battered women's hotline was displayed at the bottom."—Dena Shottenkirk, "Making Domestic Violence Public."[43]

The pauperization of motherhood spells the pauperization of childhood. Twenty percent of all children in the United States live beneath the official poverty line, the highest percentage of any industrialized country. Politicians from both mainstream political parties, echoed by the media, have blamed the values of single mothers for the increasing impoverishment of their children. Yet it was the economic crisis, with its impact on earnings, that played the most important role in generating poverty.

Women can receive income from three sources: (1) working for pay or owning property that yields investment income, (2) sharing in the income earned by other family or household members, and (3) the government. During the 1980s, women's increased access to income from paid work was offset by their decreased access to income from other family members—both because men's earnings, on average, were falling and because more and more women lived in households without a male wage earner. In order to help them survive, some women were forced to turn to the government for assistance. But this brought them little relief, and the next chapter looks at the government's priorities during these years of crisis to understand why women were unable to obtain support from state programs.

5

FROM POOR TO RICH, FROM WOMEN TO MEN: RESTRUCTURING THE STATE

Faced with falling wages, high unemployment, and an increased workload, the majority of working women had to struggle to balance work and home. By adding work hours, women barely maintained their families' income and standard of living. At the same time, the success of conservative policies meant that women faced a government determined to strip away the safety net that supported their high-wire balancing act. The figure of Anita Hill testifying in front of an all-white and all-male Senate Judiciary Committee powerfully symbolized the degree to which the government failed to meet women's needs and respond to their demands.

Beginning in the middle of the 1970s, the government's financial capacity, and political willingness, to address the needs of the population diminished. By the 1980s, state programs were being cut back in order to bolster corporate profits and to punish women who were seen to have deviated from traditional family models. Even though women were gaining increasing access to the political arena, they were unable to halt the conservative advance.

This chapter begins with a brief overview of the ways in which relationships between workers, the government, and industry were restructured and affected by the economic crisis. Next, we turn to the different ways in which women relate to the government, illustrating how in every dimension, the crisis diminished women's access to, and benefits from, government programs.

ECONOMIC CRISIS AND GOVERNMENT CRISIS

In a capitalist economy, the government tries to balance the interests of business and labor. On the one hand, demands for public spending—such as on roads, education, or health—grow continuously in an advanced capitalist country. Public spending is also needed to support the economy. Since the Great Depression, the government has been committed to an ever increasing level of spending—particularly on the military—in order to ensure that there will be a market for private sector goods and services. Thus government spending becomes a necessity for the maintenance of the "free market" economy itself.

From the Great Depression until the 1980s, the government spent primarily on infrastructure and the military, both of which had the support of both business and labor. High levels of spending were possible because the postwar boom generated sufficient revenues to enable the government to spend without upsetting industry by raising taxes. Most often, it was the working class that was taxed in order to pay for new spending. The government was able to take on a number of functions that were aimed at raising the standard of living of its citizens. Social Security, established during the 1930s, was broadened to include more workers, and in 1972 benefits were indexed so that they would rise with the cost of living. Aid to higher education expanded dramatically, beginning with the GI bill and culminating with the development of a large community college network and a set of financial aid programs that together broadened access. In addition, the public began to demand such nonmilitary "public goods" as clean air and water, safe jobs, and affirmative action—all of which cost the government and business. Organizations formed that pressured the state to meet their demands. For instance, during the late 1960s and early 1970s, the National Welfare Rights Organization (NWRO) successfully pushed for an expansion in welfare eligibility and an increase in the level of benefits.

But all these items came with a price tag. Growing programs required either a growing economy or higher tax rates, and as the economic crisis deepened, companies were increasingly called on to help foot the bill. From the capitalist point of view, these social programs contained an additional expense: any increase in the social safety net enhances labor's bargaining power. If workers can count on pensions, for instance, they are far more likely to retire early, creating a labor shortage that could drive wages up. In addition, social programs such as welfare and unemployment insurance, like the minimum wage, keep wages up since workers will not take jobs that pay any less. And workers who know they can fall back on these programs are more likely to resist dangerous working conditions and to risk organizing unions.

As their profits began to drop in the early years of the crisis, many corporations decided that public spending had to be reduced. At first they mounted direct attacks on the programs they most disliked, but in each case the constituency mobilized to protect its program. In 1971, for instance, the Nixon administration was forced to retreat from a welfare reform plan (called the Family Assistance Plan, or FAP) in the face of demonstrations by angry NWRO members brandishing placards that said "Zap FAP."

Frustrated by their lack of progress, conservatives then tried to cut government spending by cutting the tax revenues that were its lifeblood. This strategy offered a dual solution to the problem of low profits. First, it would lower corporate taxes and boost after-tax profits. Second, legislatures at all levels of government, faced with declining tax revenues, would be unable to expand government programs, and would even, if tax cutting was successful enough, be forced to make cuts. The beauty of the plan lay in the fact that a tax cut appealed to everyone, even those who would in the end suffer the most from it. Instead of having to fight constituencies mobilized to protect their pet programs, the pro-business forces could bask in widespread support for their tax-cutting agenda.

The tax revolt, as it came to be called, began at the state level, with attacks on the property tax. While these tax-cutting referenda and ballot initiatives were sold to the public as a way to ease the burden of property taxes on the poor and on retirees living on fixed incomes, the greatest beneficiaries were businesses. Corporate property tax bills fell sharply, while most owners of residential property faced ever rising bills.

By 1980, the business community felt that a change in political leadership and public policy was needed because the Democratic administration of Jimmy Carter was not acting in their interests. But if the Democrats were to be thrown out, working class voters had to be persuaded that the spending on public goods was to blame for their economic problems. "Are you better off?" asked Ronald Reagan. And the working class, eager for someone to blame for rising unemployment and capital flight, turned to the Republican Party.

Reagan promised the electorate "across the board" tax cuts, a promise that drew working-class families that had always voted Democratic into the Reagan coalition. But the actual plan that was enacted in 1981 offered substantially more dollars of tax relief

Figure 5-1

Composition of Federal Outlays, 1980 and 1987

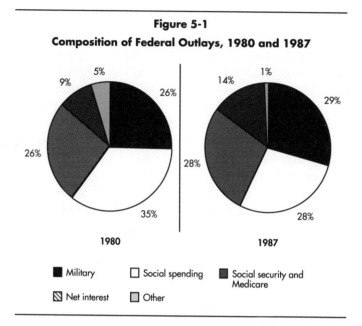

Military   ☐ Social spending   ☒ Social security and Medicare

☒ Net interest   ☐ Other

to the rich than to the poor. In fact, taxes were actually *raised* for three out of four families. In 1991, the Congressional Budget Office found that all but the very richest (the top 5 percent) and the very poorest (the bottom 20 percent) were paying a larger share of their incomes in federal taxes than they had been before Reagan.[1] At the same time, reductions in corporate taxes added to a dramatic decline in federal revenues. This was accompanied by the largest peacetime military buildup in the history of the nation (see Figure 5-1). The federal government was forced to borrow to pay its way, and borrowing jumped from 15 percent to 30 percent of total federal spending (see Figure 5-2). In 1992, for instance, a Washington-based organization, Citizens for Tax Justice, estimated that the government would lose approximately $84 billion in tax revenues not paid by the top 1 percent of the income distribution. In addition, the government must pay interest on *previous* borrowing that was necessitated by the tax cuts, estimated at another $81 billion. This interest must be paid because in every year since the tax cuts were enacted the federal government has borrowed to make up for lost revenues.[2]

The stage was set for the budget crisis of the 1980s. As reduced revenues led to the impoverishment of the public sector, political pressure to do something about the federal deficit grew. And if nothing could be done on the income side, it had to be done on the expense side. Defense spending was cut back somewhat, but Congress and the President were unwilling to make really deep cuts: they were only able to reduce the *rate* of increase, not the level of spending itself. Compared to fiscal year 1980, for instance, the government spent 10 percent more on defense and 83 percent more on the national debt in 1990. The three items in the federal budget that have increased the most since 1980 are interest on the debt, the savings and loan bailout, and defense spending (see Figure 5-3).

WOMEN AS TAXPAYERS

The tax cuts enacted during the Reagan years favored the wealthy at the expense of poor and moderate income people. Since women living alone and women supporting families on their own disproportionately fall into these last two categories, few of the tax cut dollars came their way.

One rationale behind the tax cuts was that they would encourage people to work harder: if workers took home a larger share of their paychecks, they would work longer hours. Ironically, however, it was low-income women, who received few tax breaks, who increased their work effort, working longer hours and even taking on additional jobs; high-income women, who did receive tax relief, did *not* work harder. The incentive for low-income women was not tax cuts, however, but the steady erosion in pay and benefits.

The effect of the federal tax cuts has rippled down through the tax system. One of the first acts of the Reagan administration was

---

Figure 5-2

How We Paid for Federal Spending, 1970 and 1990

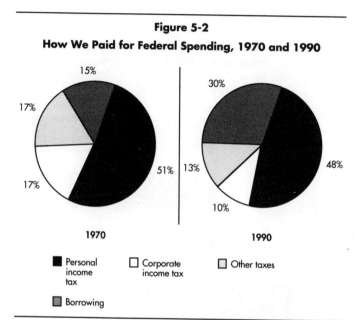

Personal income tax · Corporate income tax · Other taxes · Borrowing

---

to eliminate revenue sharing, a federal program that gave back some of the federal tax revenues to state governments. Once this happened, the states faced their own financial crisis, caught between demands for tax cuts by state residents (whose appetite for "no new taxes" had been whetted by Reagan administration rhetoric) and the need for greater tax revenues because of the loss of federal funds. Many states were forced to raise taxes, but most did this not by increasing the income tax but by raising sales taxes. Because they are a flat percentage tax, rather than one that rises as earnings increase, sales taxes take proportionately more from the poor than the rich. They are called *regressive* taxes, while the graduated income tax is called a *progressive* tax. As state and local governments increased their tax rates, low-income households saw their tax burdens increase. In 1991, for instance, households with total incomes under $10,000 paid 10.7 percent of their income in sales and excise taxes. In contrast, the average family

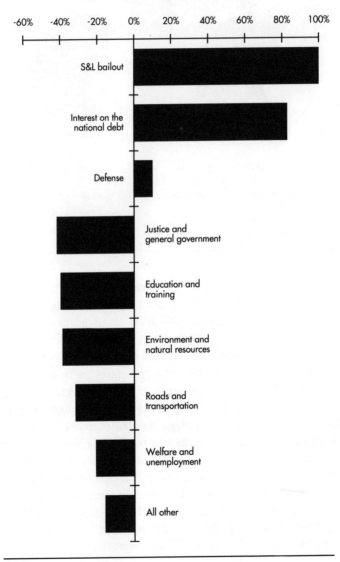

Figure 5-3

**Percent Changes in Federal Spending
from Fiscal 1980 to Fiscal 1990**

paid only 4.4 percent of its income in such taxes. Women who maintain their own households, particularly older women and women with small children, pay a disproportionately large percentage of their incomes in sales tax because they have lower incomes than men maintaining households on their own or living in married-couple families. The shift to a regressive tax meant that the tax burden shifted from more affluent families to low and moderate income families.[3] Thus women not only gained less from the reduction in federal income taxes, but they were hurt more by state and local tax increases. At the same time, the federal government raised the payroll tax, a tax that is also highly regressive. Women, because they are disproportionately concentrated among low-wage earners, were also hardest hit by the payroll tax increase.

WOMEN AS RECIPIENTS OF ASSISTANCE

Women receive income from the government through a variety of programs. Perhaps the most discussed in recent years has been Aid to Families with Dependent Children (AFDC), the leading cash benefit program for the poor. AFDC is partly funded by the federal government and partly by the states, which determine benefit levels and eligibility. Beginning in the mid-1970s, the tax revolt at the state and local level began to force states to cut back on many programs, including AFDC, so that benefits failed to keep up with the rate of inflation. In 1981, Congress passed a Reagan initiative that cut 444,000 AFDC recipients off the rolls and lowered benefits for another several hundred thousand. Since 1973, the number of people on the welfare rolls has remained fairly constant (see Figure 5-4), even though the number of poor women and children has increased. As a result, the share of those in need who actually receive welfare has fallen. In 1973, 81 out of every 100 children in poverty received AFDC; by 1989, that ratio had fallen to 58 out of 100. In addition, by the early Reagan years there had already been substantial erosion in

Figure 5-4

**Average Number of AFDC Recipients, 1970–1990
(in millions)**

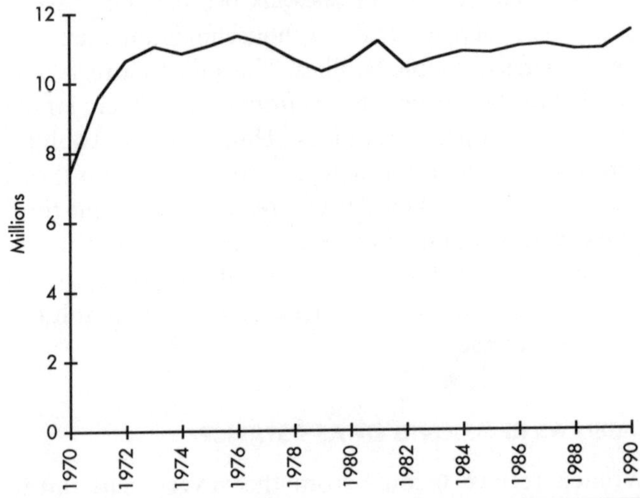

the purchasing power of AFDC benefits (see Figure 5-5), and that decline continued.[4]

Much of the decline in numbers came about because states tightened eligibility restrictions. In 1985, for instance, the Southern Regional Project on Infant Mortality found that the number of families denied AFDC benefits on procedural grounds had reached 1.5 million, up 75 percent from 1980.[6] These procedural grounds included an inability to provide adequate documentation or to fill out the application form correctly. Forms are long (in some states they are fifty pages), and recipients are usually asked to provide extensive proof of their economic and family status, including pay stubs, Social Security cards for all family members, bank statements, proof of residency, children's birth certificates, and rent and utility receipts. The income limits are very low: in twenty-nine states, income at *60*

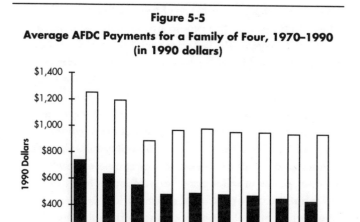

Figure 5-5

**Average AFDC Payments for a Family of Four, 1970–1990
(in 1990 dollars)**

percent of the federal poverty level will make a family of three ineligible for AFDC. (In 1990, that would mean that a family of three, consisting of one parent with two children, would be ineligible if its income were over $527 a month!) In addition, if applicants have assets above the federal limits ($1000 in cash and $1500 equity in a car), they are declared ineligible.

A Welfare Mother in California. "When Sonia Blutgarten spent $20 for cake mix and party favors to celebrate her sons' birthdays, it meant she could not afford to do eight loads of wash. The fat sacks of dirty clothes crowded the corridor of her shabby apartment for months while she squirreled away a dollar here and a dollar there to finance a trip to the laundry. For Ms. Blutgarten, a 29-

year-old unemployed mother of two, such trade-offs are
a fact of life, part of the day-to-day calculus of supporting herself, 6-year-old TeAndre and 4-year-old Kehnan
on a $663 monthly welfare check, plus $168 worth of
food stamps.... Even with the current benefits, the fourth
most generous among all states, Ms. Blutgarten rarely
reaches the end of the month in the black, despite care-
ful budgeting and much juggling of priorities, after she
has paid her $400 rent and her $60 utility bill. She rides
an hour and a half on the bus every couple of weeks to
buy four packs of toilet paper at $.69 each, less than
half what it costs at the local supermarket. She has been
rationing an inch of window cleaner left behind by a previous tenant because there will be no more when that is
gone. And things are getting worse for Ms. Blutgarten, a
high-school dropout. State budget cuts are expected to
reduce services by MediCal, the state health plan for the
poor, which has been whittled down in recent years.
And city budget cuts in San Francisco forced up the price
of a monthly transit pass to $40 from $35. Ms. Blutgarten is one of three welfare mothers who a few months
ago sued the California Department of Social Services, ac-
cusing the department of failing to comply with federal
regulations requiring states to reevaluate welfare
benefits every three years. The suit, brought with the
help of an advocacy group, is still pending."—Jane
Gross, "On the Edge of Poverty in California."[5]

It is no accident that AFDC eligibility has been so severely
restricted. During the 1980s, the corporate cost-cutting agenda
demanded that wages fall wherever possible, and the shift from
manufacturing to services required a labor force that was willing
to work for little money and few benefits. Welfare mothers were
a potential pool of low-wage labor, but they had many problems

to overcome if they were to go out and work. In 1988, Congress enacted a sweeping federal welfare reform proposal, called the Family Support Act, that requires states to provide welfare-to-work programs that it is hoped will increase the incentive to work for pay. States must offer at least two of the following four activities: help to individuals and groups in finding jobs, work supplementation (a subsidy to bring low wages up to federal minimums), on-the-job training programs, and workfare (a mandatory work program). Funds are available for supportive services, including childcare, but levels of funding and the quality of these programs vary widely.

The act was intended to solve a problem that policy makers believed had grown worse throughout the 1960s and 1970s. In popular language, it was argued that welfare recipients had become "dependent" on the system, that they were staying poor in order to receive benefits. However, there is little conclusive evidence that such a "crisis of dependency" existed. The majority of public assistance recipients use the system as a temporary support during periods of family crisis or transition. Over 50 percent of those on welfare stay for less than two years, and 62 percent for less than four years.[7] Approximately 75 percent of welfare recipients apply for assistance because of a family event, such as a divorce, a separation, or the birth of a child. Once their life circumstances have stabilized, they leave the rolls: the most common route out of AFDC is another family event (marriage or the maturing of dependent children). Only 15 percent of welfare spells begin with a drop in family earnings that is unrelated to a change in family structure.

There is no conclusive evidence that the welfare system changes attitudes and behaviors in ways that create dependency and undermine the motivation to work, and researchers have found no evidence that children who grow up in welfare families "pass on" welfare dependence to their children.[8] According to the Department of Education, each year a child lives in poverty increases the likelihood that she or he will fall behind a grade level in school.[9] Thus adequate incomes for poor families are, in and of themselves, a long-term anti-poverty measure.

Those recipients who do not leave the rolls quickly differ in important ways from those who do. They have low levels of formal education (47 percent of AFDC recipients do not have a high school diploma), or live in areas where paid employment opportunities are scarce, child care is unavailable, and transportation difficult.[10] Many have children who need full-time care. (In fact, national data show that poor children are almost *twice* as likely to suffer from severe functional disabilities as children in families with higher incomes.)[11] Many long-term welfare recipients are teen parents who drop out of school to have children and have no realistic chance of making a living wage. In Illinois, for instance, the Young Parents' Program found that 25 percent of parents under age 21 receiving AFDC were unable to participate in any education, training, or job programs because of urgent family problems.[12] Mandatory work programs will not solve these problems or provide adequate incomes for these families.[13]

Even if they are able to overcome these barriers and find jobs, single mothers usually earn far too little to support a family adequately. Women find it difficult to "work their way off welfare" because the program cuts them off at very low income levels, preventing them from combining work and welfare in the short run, in order to move off welfare altogether in the longer run. In addition, as incomes increase, food stamps, Medicaid, and the Earned Income Tax Credit become unavailable, while work expenses and taxes rise. In Pennsylvania, for instance, an increase in *earned* income from $2,000 to $10,000 led to almost *no* increase in disposable income (income available to be spent, after subtracting these work expenses and taxes).

Discussions of welfare in the United States have always been silently dominated by issues of race. However, beginning in the 1980s, the discussion merged with powerful anti-tax sentiments and a resurgence of racism (both in corporate America and among white working-class constituencies) to provide new political opportunities for politicians willing to play the "welfare card." White voters became convinced that their taxes had increased because of the generous welfare benefits paid out to black recipients, and that this had happened because politicians, particularly in the Democratic Party, had pandered to the demands of black voters. This politics of resentment, and the racial polarization that came with it, helped elect both Ronald Reagan and George Bush to the White House, but neither party is innocent in the attack on welfare recipients. For the Republicans, to attack welfare is to attack government overspending on the poor. For the Democrats, welfare reform is necessary to show that they can be efficient managers and to avoid the "tax-and-spend" label. Neither party has the courage to defend either the redistributive or safety-net aspects of AFDC—the fact that it gives income to the poor and stabilizes spending in recessions. Thus in the absence of a strong movement among welfare recipients themselves, AFDC remains vulnerable. In the 1991 wave of state fiscal crises, for instance, thirty states froze AFDC benefits and several others either reduced them or announced plans to do so.

Welfare Rights Movement Revives. "The welfare rights movement, an important source of change in the 1960s and 1970s, was revived in June 1987 when welfare mothers and organizers formed a National Welfare Rights Union (NWRU) 'to re-dedicate ourselves to the pursuit of social justice for all members of our society, particularly those have been excluded from the benefits of this nation.' Organized and led by the poor themselves, NWRU's first annual convention in September 1988 drew over 100 people from 18 states.... Welfare mothers are on the move for higher grants in many

places. Massachusetts welfare mothers and their sup-
porters launched one of the first Up and Out of Poverty
Campaigns in 1984. Targeting the courts, the legislature
and the streets, their creative tactics drew a lot of media
coverage and led to welfare grant hikes. Among other
things, the activists held a Thanksgiving dinner contrast-
ing with that of a rich family, slept over at the State
House to emphasize the lack of shelter, and conducted a
mock funeral that tied low welfare benefits to high infant mortality rates. Broadening the issue, they
presented Hog awards to top banks and corporations
that paid little or no taxes, thereby linking tax breaks
for the rich to the suffering of the poor.... In Brooklyn,
NY, activists organized families living in welfare hotels
to protect their rights and to fight for permanent housing, one time barricading themselves in the social service
office at the hotel.... In New Hampshire, Parents for Justice and others ... helped to create an independent state
commission to determine the real costs of raising
children.... In St. Louis, Missouri, the Reform Organization of Welfare uses a welfare simulation project to educate the public about life on public assistance. Some of
the welfare rights groups ... publish their own
newspapers and magazines, which describe their work,
analyze the issues, and help welfare mothers 'negotiate'
the welfare system."—Mimi Abramovitz, "Low Income
Women's Activism."[14]

WOMEN AS CONSUMERS OF PUBLIC SERVICES

Since women are, on average, poorer than men, they rely
disproportionately on government programs to meet their needs
in such areas as housing, health care, food, and cash income. The
Coalition on Women and the Budget estimated early in the

Reagan term that women headed 94 percent of all families that received AFDC and made up 60 percent of all Medicaid recipients, 85 percent of Food Stamp recipients, and 67 percent of all legal services clients.[15] Not surprisingly, cuts to public services disproportionately affected women. Among these were cuts to AFDC, student financial aid, child nutrition (down 28 percent in 1981 alone) assistance in housing construction (down 80 percent), Food Stamps, employment and training programs (down 40 percent between 1981 and 1985), and funding for community health services. A variety of programs under the Social Services Block Grant were devastated by a cut of nearly 25 percent between 1981 and 1985; the grant provides federal monies to states for day care, services for victims of domestic violence, and services for homebound disabled people.

Women were not targeted by these cuts, but they ended up suffering the most. For instance, housing expenditures for low-income people were cut roughly 80 percent between 1980 and 1990—conservatives argued that the private market would do a much better job of supplying housing than the government. The construction of new public housing came to a halt and spending to renovate existing housing was not enough to make up for the deterioration in the existing housing stock. Cuts in housing expenditures affected women disproportionately because they are more likely to be residents of public housing than men. The administration shifted its emphasis to rent subsidies and housing vouchers, which sent low-income families into the private market to seek housing. But there women face substantial discrimination. Between 1977 and 1980, the Department of Housing and Urban Development had helped 422,000 households each year; during the Reagan administration, that number fell to 155,000.[16] In contrast, housing subsidies for the middle class and wealthy— the most important of which is mortgage interest deductions for homeowners—soared from $11 billion in 1976 to $53 billion in 1989. Roughly 75 percent of these deductions went to people in the top 15 percent of the income distribution. Since female-headed households are far less likely to be at the top rungs of the economic ladder, they are far less likely to be homeowners and far less likely to receive this federal subsidy.

Cuts in Medicaid (for the poor) and Medicare (for all those over age 65) also had a disproportionate effect on women. For instance, the increase in co-payments—the amount a patient pays herself—was particularly burdensome to low-income people. Since the majority of the elderly poor are women, they were hit the hardest by these increases.

Women were also disproportionately affected by the non-monetary effects of the budget cuts. For instance, the Reagan administration introduced a new method of reimbursement to hospitals for the care they provided older and poor people under Medicaid and Medicare that limited the amount paid for each procedure or operation. If a hospital spent more than that amount, it had to absorb the difference—for example, if the limit for an appendectomy was set at $5,000 for a three-day stay but the patient stayed for ten days, the hospital would only be reimbursed for the first three days, or $5,000. This created an incentive for hospitals to discharge patients "sicker and quicker."

On the surface this saved the federal government money. However, who cares for these patients when they come home? When patients are discharged early, it is the women in the household who are most likely to bear the burden of their care. In 1982, for instance, nearly 75 percent of the over 2 million people providing care for disabled or chronically ill people over 65 were women.[17] These cuts, although driven by the desire to control costs, only *shifted* the costs from one party (the government) to another. These caregivers not only lose their leisure time, but they may also lose their jobs. During the early years of the Bush administration, a bill was introduced into Congress that would have required employers to provide unpaid family leave to parents of newborns and newly adopted children, or to workers who needed time off to care for a family member who was seriously ill. Bush vetoed the bill, arguing that it would hurt

U.S. businesses to offer parental leave because they couldn't afford to hire temporary workers.

Health Care: We Gotta Have It! "MADRE, a New York-based women's organization working on issues of women's health since 1983, has declared national health care a priority. Through the HEALTH CARE: WE GOTTA HAVE IT! Campaign, diverse women across the country are organizing to educate themselves, frame the debate in women-relevant terms, and demand our right to adequate health care.... [The Campaign], a new coalition of women's groups, is laying plans for an unprecedented National Women's Convergence on universal health care in 1993. Through a series of speak-outs in every region of the country, culminating with a national convention, this multi-racial, cross-class coalition will help articulate and advocate a women's platform for universal health care.... We must see to it, for example, that the package of legislation that is finally passed includes access to the full range of reproductive and family planning services.... As society's primary caregivers, women are the unacknowledged experts on the medical system's failure. More and more of us are unable to afford prenatal or maternity care, doctor's visits for sick children, mammograms, pap smears, long-term care for aging relatives, or a host of other basic services. Women also have a vision from the ground up of what health and medical care should provide."—Francisca Cavazos and Laura Flanders, "Women Come Together for National Health Care."[18]

DEREGULATING AND REREGULATING WOMEN

Women were also the victims of the Reagan-Bush effort to deregulate the economy—to reduce the number and strength of the laws that regulate businesses. During the 1970s, for instance, a whole range of civil rights programs that were supposed to create new opportunities for white women and for people of color were developed. A federal agency, the Equal Employment Opportunity Commission (EEOC), was created to hear sex and race discrimination complaints and to file lawsuits against the discriminators. Another agency, the Office of Federal Contract Compliance, required companies doing business with the government to file plans that showed how they intended to meet affirmative action guidelines for hiring and promoting groups that had been discriminated against in the past. To the extent that these antidiscrimination policies have been applied, they have made gains possible that would otherwise not have occurred.[19]

Yet all these affirmative action programs were gutted during the Reagan years. The laws creating the agencies were not repealed and the agencies themselves were not dismantled. Instead, people who were opposed to the agencies' purposes were appointed to head them. One example was Clarence Thomas, an avowed opponent of affirmative action, who was appointed to head the EEOC (Thomas is now a Supreme Court Justice). During his tenure, the agency closed cases without full investigation, failed to seek adequate monetary awards, undermined the use of comparable worth, and delayed implementation of the Age Discrimination in Employment Act.[20] Other agencies also worked to destroy antidiscrimination policies.[21]

In other areas of regulation, such as occupational safety and health, the Reagan administration cut staffing and enforcement, and lowered or failed to set safety standards. Under Bush, the Occupational Safety and Health Administration (OSHA) failed to formulate standards to prevent carpal tunnel syndrome, a disabling condition that strikes workers who must perform rapid, repetitive movements with their fingers and hands. Factory operatives are most prone to this injury, which has claimed a rising number of victims as the speed of the assembly line has increased. In chicken-processing plants, for example, workers must cut chickens between 60 and 90 times a minute. Over the past decade, rising demand for chicken and increasing competition in the industry have sped up the pace of the assembly line by as much as 60 percent. Journalist Barbara Goldoftas, who has studied what are called cumulative trauma disorders, or CTDs, points out:

> The sudden jump in CTDs in part reflects greater awareness of diseases that were once ignored. In industries like automaking, textiles, meatpacking, and poultry, where rates have always been high, unions and workers advocacy groups have been publicizing the risks of CTDs.... Injury rates have [also] soared in postal work, data entry, and journalism, for example, where they were uncommon before. Some of this rise stems from new technologies and changes in the design of work.[22]

In 1990, faced with overwhelming evidence that meatpacking workers (predominantly male) were suffering above-average rates of crippling and painful injuries as a result of the design of the job, OSHA finally issued guidelines for the industry. But the guidelines were only voluntary, and OSHA has yet to address the problems faced by women in fields such as data entry and poultry processing.

The deregulation agenda did not, however, extend to women's reproductive choices, where the government sought to limit and control women's lives. One area where the Reagan and Bush administrations regulated rather than deregulated was access to abortion, particularly for poor women. Although antiabortion groups want to make abortions illegal, they have not been able to achieve this. But by making abortions less available, they have made them more expensive.

Paying for Choice. "Faced with higher priced abortions and a lack of public funding, poor women need more time to raise the necessary funds. Delaying the procedure ... increases both the costs and the health risks. Abortions performed in the eleventh or twelfth week of pregnancy are three times more dangerous than abortions performed in the eighth week, and the risks increase as the pregnancy progresses. The average fee for an abortion performed in a clinic within the first 12 weeks of pregnancy was $247 [in 1989], while the average price soared to $697 for an abortion at 20 weeks of pregnancy.... Women will have to pick up other costs of limited access to abortion services,... [such as] transportation and possibly accommodation costs.... Up to 80 percent raise the money to pay for an abortion themselves. To pay for the procedure, many buy less food or clothing or let other bills go unpaid; a majority report that the abortion was a serious financial hardship.... As a result of public funding bans ... 20 percent of the women who would have received a Medicaid-funded abortion in 1980 carried their unwanted pregnancy to full term."—Randy Albelda, "Aborting Choice."[23]

THE ANTI-WOMAN STATE

Women were an easy target for these cuts because they have little political power, not only because they are underrepresented but also because women are more likely to be poor and the affluent have more electoral power than the poor. According to journalists Sidney Blumenthal and Thomas Byrne Edsall,

Since 1960 and 1964, the disparity in voter-turnout rates between the top third of the income distribution and those in the bottom third has grown from a roughly 25-point difference to a 40-point spread. In other words, just those voters on whom the Democratic Party has come increasingly to depend for large margins—those in the bottom third of the income distribution—are those whose turnout rates have dropped the most, while the affluent, who have become increasingly Republican, have continued to go to the polls at relatively high levels.[24]

Women's political power has also been limited by what journalist Susan Faludi calls a "backlash" against the feminist gains of the 1970s. In her prize-winning book, *Backlash*, Faludi shows how the media has both exaggerated the 1970s and 1980s as periods of dramatic gains for women and undermined those gains by focusing on women's problems:

> How can women be in so much trouble at the same time that they are supposed to be so blessed? If the status of women has never been higher, why is their emotional state so low? If women got what they asked for, what could possibly be the matter now? The prevailing wisdom of the past decade has supported one, and only one, answer to this riddle: it must be all that equality that's causing all that pain.... The women's movement, as we are told time and again, has proved women's own worst enemy.[25]

By attacking the women's movement, Faludi points out, this new "prevailing wisdom" diminishes the possibility of organized response to the government's attack on women. At the same time, the media buries stories of women's efforts to organize to counter the effects of the economic crisis and government policies. But in fact the crisis has mobilized women across the country to organize among themselves, in coalitions with men, with multiracial groups, and with people overseas.

Recapturing the State for the People. "One steamy afternoon last July, Mayor Emma Gresham [of Keysville, Georgia] was walking toward her office when her assistant intercepted her with the good news: Keysville had just won a $400,000 federal grant to provide indoor plumbing to local residents.... For most small Georgia towns, getting a water grant would hardly qualify as a remarkable event.... But Keysville is not an ordinary town. Just five years ago, it wasn't a town at all, its local government having been disbanded by whites during the Great Depression.... But in 1985, black residents pulled together to resurrect their community.... Gresham took the lead in a self-help organization of black residents called Keysville Concerned Citizens who were struggling to improve living conditions. For nearly two decades, the church-based group had been selling chicken dinners to raise money for community improvements.... [To achieve more improvements] Keysville Concerned Citizens pushed for local elections. In 1985, six black residents ran for office unopposed, and were sworn in as the new mayor and town council of Keysville. But white residents, fearing that the new government would levy taxes to pay for city services, went to court [and won].... When new elections were held in 1988, black residents were prepared. They handed out leaflets and held town meetings and worked with the American Civil Liberties Union and Christic Institute South, a social justice group based in North Carolina.... After another year of legal wrangling, the U.S. Supreme Court ... cleared the way for Keysville to hold another election in 1989. This time, Gresham beat white opponent J. Upton Cochran by 59 votes and blacks won all five council seats."—Frederick D. Robinson, "Keys to the City."[26]

FROM A POLITICS OF SURVIVAL
TO A POLITICS OF TRANSFORMATION

Writing in 1930, the Italian philosopher Antonio Gramsci characterized a crisis as a period in which the old ways are dying but the new are not yet born. In the current crisis, many of the old institutions that once ensured U.S. economic growth have disintegrated, but new institutions have not yet arisen to take their place.[27] Today, in the United States, we find ourselves at such a moment.

The disintegration of institutions that were so successful in promoting growth for decades has opened the way for political warfare among alternative visions of the way out of the crisis, and much of contemporary political and social life can be interpreted as a struggle among these visions. The rise of the conservative wing of the Republican Party, for instance, represents business's attempt to put forward its vision. Jesse Jackson's 1988 bid for the presidency represented a progressive alternative. Even the voter discontent of the 1992 campaign represents a desire for an alternative not yet envisioned.

The Conservative Vision

For the past twelve years, conservatives have attempted to restore capitalist profitability through a set of policies that restructured the workplace, the home, and the state. Their policies have lowered wages, diminishing the collective power of workers, transferred government activities to households (particularly to women), and shifted the burden of taxation to low and moderate-income households. To achieve those ends, conservatives undertook a political strategy that blamed unions, workers of color, and women, along with welfare state policies and government regulation, for the crisis.

If they succeed—and the election of a Democratic administration does not mean that the conservative effort is over, only that it has shifted its center of activities—the world will be far from the "kinder, gentler" place promised by George Bush. Inequality will increase, undermining social solidarity across race-ethnicity, gender, sexual orientation, and other social divisions. The gaps between whites and people of color will grow, reversing decades of progress. The gap between married couples and other households will increase as neither the government nor the labor market provide adequate income to women maintaining households. The gap between those at the top of the labor hierarchy and those at the bottom will increase, creating greater polarization within groups: the life experiences of affluent and poor African Americans will increasingly diverge; women corporate lawyers will have less and less in common with their secretaries; the pensions of retired workers will be slashed by corporations claiming they need the funds to pay for current workers' health insurance. The cities and the suburbs, already two different worlds, will become even more radically separate and opposed, segregated by race-ethnicity, by class, and by life-opportunities. And those at the top will increasingly defend themselves against those at the bottom with violence and repression.

The Progressive Alternative

Fortunately, there is an alternative to this nightmarish scenario. In the alternative scenario, the goal is to raise the standard of living of workers, not to lower it. Worker productivity is increased through investments in education, training, health care, and childcare, while wages rise as workers are guaranteed job security, retraining, and collective bargaining rights. Workers are involved in all the decisions affecting their communities and their workplaces, including decisions over technology and environmental impact. Affirmative action policies guarantee that discriminatory practices are named and stopped.

In the home, new forms of family achieve social and political recognition. Paid parental leave and a national system of dependent care ease the burden of the double day. Child support moves toward the Swedish system, where the government advances funds to the custodial parent, regardless of the noncustodial parent's ability to pay. As the standard of living rises, more leisure time becomes available so that people can participate in family and community life.

The government provides universal programs that work toward greater equality. Progressive taxation channels the wealth of the few toward the needs of the many through universal health care, pensions, and programs in housing, education, and infrastructure. Government becomes accountable to all, rather than simply to the affluent campaign contributors, as campaign finance reform eliminates the privileges of wealth in the political arena.

But how can we possibly achieve this alternative scenario? The answer lies in the nature of crises themselves. With the collapse of the old institutions, there are new opportunities for experimentation, for changing ideologies, and for political and cultural realignments. Today, at the grassroots level, there are hundreds of thousands of groups working for progressive change, seeking to restructure the economy, the household, and the state for democratic and participatory ends. Even with a Democrat in the White House, these groups will need to continue to press government and business for social change.

Some groups are organizing in ways that bring together new constituencies, often constituencies that the conservative movement is attempting to pit against one another. For instance, workers in different countries have begun to come together to address common issues and to resist business's attempt to divide and conquer. These new international coalitions alert one another to potential plant movements, support one another's strikes, and share information on job safety and environmental issues.

To counter the conservative division of "taxpayer against recipient," new coalitions protesting budget cutbacks have united community members and state workers, such as human services providers and their clients, teachers and their students. These new groups, many of them led by women defending programs that benefit themselves and their children, have also turned their attention to the tax side of government budgets, identifying progressive tax proposals and linking them with the need to maintain public services.

Another aspect of grassroots organizing against the effects of economic crisis radically alters the inner workings of older institutions, such as labor unions, or practices, such as wage determination. To organize women, people of color, and immigrants, unions have developed creative tactics, often reminiscent of the civil rights movement, such as sit-ins, demonstrations, use of the media, and direct appeals to consumers of goods and services. The new union movement addresses family and worklife issues, job safety issues, and the relationship between the community and the workplace by providing childcare centers, as well as classes in adult literacy and English as a second language. Rather than permit the underground economy to grow and exploit ever more women and immigrants, unions are attempting to organize sweatshops from the border towns of Mexico to the garment shops of New York and Los Angeles. New organizing drives in hotels and restaurants, universities, and the public sector are democratic, inviting all workers to participate in decision-making and in collective bargaining.

The comparable worth movement has challenged traditional practices of wage determination, in which the history of race- and sex-typing of jobs continues to drag down women's wages and those of people of color. Pay equity plans, developed as a result of pressure from unions, women's advocacy groups, and people of color, force state and local governments and private employers to scrutinize their pay scales for race and sex bias. In the process, value judgments that place equipment over people, and financial management over human services, can be addressed and reversed.

Other forms of organizing develop and support entirely new institutions that address human needs in radically different ways. Bargaining with private employers and with city and state governments, unmarried heterosexual couples and gay and lesbian couples are demanding coverage under health and pension plans equal to that provided to married couples. New forms of employment, such as worker ownership, are challenging capital's right to create and define jobs. Some worker-owned firms have been created to save jobs when a business is on the brink of bankruptcy or its owners no longer wish to operate it. Others are entirely new efforts, redesigning working conditions in a way that meets the needs of both the workers and the larger community.

What do all these efforts have in common? They create collective possibilities for analyzing the causes of the crisis and overturning existing relationships of exploitation and domination. They bring people together across lines of race, ethnicity, gender, and sexual orientation in ways that include those the conservatives have scapegoated and that therefore reject the politics of division. They are democratic to their core, involving people at the grassroots in the decisions that affect their lives.

In each of these areas, described above and elsewhere in this book, women have taken the lead. Creative strategies have been developed by women of color, poor women, lesbians, and disabled women. Perhaps this is because these women have been so severely affected by the crisis, forced to assume new burdens of work and responsibility but deprived of safety nets and guarantees. Perhaps, caught in the crisis, women have been able to see it more clearly than those whose privileges have insulated them from its worst effects. And finally, perhaps it is the very diversity of women's experiences that has given them a vision of alternative possibilities that is richer, more pluralistic, and more democratic. At this moment of crisis, when the old framework is dead, women are giving birth to the new.

NOTES

CHAPTER 1: WOMEN AND ECONOMIC CRISIS

1. During the long postwar boom, Dr. M. Harvey Brenner of Johns Hopkins University calculated some of the human costs of an economic slowdown. He found, for instance, that an increase in overall unemployment for six years increases the number of deaths by approximately 37,000, and increases admissions to state mental hospitals and prisons by over 7,000. Since then, the effects of economic slowdown have been much more widespread and more severe, particularly in the 1980s, when the government safety net was shredded by conservative economic policies. As a result, Brenner's estimates clearly underestimate the true costs of the current crisis. See a description of Brenner's work in Barry Bluestone and Bennett Harrison, *The Deindustrialization of America: Plant Closings, Community Abandonment, and the Dismantling of Basic Industry* (New York: Basic Books, 1982), pp. 63-66.

2. Barbara Barnett, "Ina Mae Best: Union Grade," *In These Times* 15, 1 May 1991, p. 4.

3. Peter T. Kilborn, "Lives of Unexpected Poverty in Center of a Land of Plenty," *New York Times,* 7 July 1992.

4. Louise Palmer, "Stand-off in the Sweatshops," *The Progressive* (May 1991).
5. Stephanie Strom, "Fashion Avenue's $100 Million Woman," *New York Times*, 17 May 1992.
6. The line between these two roles is sometimes blurred, as when a domestic servant is paid to take care of someone else's family, or when a woman runs a small business out of her own home.
7. This quote, and the material in the following pages, is drawn from Teresa Amott and Julie Matthaei, *Race, Gender, and Work: A Multicultural Economic History of Women in the United States* (Boston: South End Press, 1991), pp. 2-3.
8. See Steven Jay Gould, *The Mismeasure of Man* (New York: W.W. Norton and Co., 1981) and Michael Omi and Howard Winant, *Racial Formation in the United States: From the 1960s to the 1980s* (New York: Routledge & Kegan Paul, 1986) for a summary of current thinking on the social construction of racial and ethnic categories.
9. I use the term "nation" here to emphasize the extent to which different Native American societies were sovereign entities, whose rights to self-determination must be recognized and respected.
10. During the seventeenth century, somewhere between one-half and two-thirds of colonial white immigrants arrived here as indentured servants. See Amott and Matthaei, *Race, Gender, and Work*, pp. 96-99.
11. Plantations in Hawaii did not involve chattel slavery. Instead, plantation owners typically hired Chinese, Japanese, or Filipino laborers as contract laborers, in a system similar to indentured servitude. Very few women were contract laborers, but some male workers brought their wives and some plantation owners imported Asian women as prostitutes or servants. In this way, Asians immigrated to Hawaii, and many eventually made their way to the continent to work on railroads, in mining, or in agriculture.
12. Amott and Matthaei, *Race, Gender, and Work*, p. 295.
13. In the Spanish language, the word "Chicanos" refers to men of Mexican origin, while the word "Chicanas" refers to women.
14. Amott and Matthaei, *Race, Gender, and Work*, p. 299. The researcher cited in the quote is Jeanne Boydston, "To Earn Her Daily Bread: Housework and Antebellum Working-Class Subsistence," *Radical History Review* 35 (April 1986): 17-19.
15. Juliet Schor, *The Overworked American* (New York: Basic Books, 1992), pp. 87-88.
16. Alice Kessler-Harris, *Out to Work: A History of Wage-Earning Women in the United States* (New York: Oxford University Press, 1982), p. 276.
17. Amott and Matthaei, *Race, Gender, and Work*, p. 316.
18. U.S. Bureau of the Census, *1970 Census of the Population: General Social and Economic Characteristics, U.S. Summary*, Table 91, p. 392.

19. U.S. Bureau of the Census, *Statistical Abstract of the United States 1988*, Table 202, p. 125.

CHAPTER 2: THE POSTWAR ECONOMY SLOWS DOWN

1. "Defining Consumer Confidence," *Dollars and Sense* (May 1992).
2. Cigdem Kurdas, "The General Picture," in *The Imperiled Economy, Book One, Macroeconomics from a Left Perspective* (New York: Union for Radical Political Economics, 1987), p. 3.
3. This section relies on the summary found in James T. Campen and Arthur MacEwan, "Crisis, Contradictions, and Conservative Controversies in Contemporary U.S. Capitalism," *RRPE* 14, no. 3 (Fall 1982): 3-7. They in turn draw from a long literature of writing on economic crisis.
4. For instance, when the prime minister of Iran, Mohammed Mossadegh, attempted to nationalize the Iranian oil industry in 1953, the United States simply installed a new head of government, the Shah, who promised to maintain good relations with the U.S. government and U.S. oil companies. Another key example of U.S. political and economic dominance involved the entire system of international finance set up after World War II. This system guaranteed a privileged role to the United States by setting up the dollar as a key reserve currency. See Fred Block, *The Origins of International Economic Disorder* (Berkeley: University of California Press, 1977).
5. Philip Mattera, *Prosperity Lost* (Reading, MA: Addison-Wesley, 1992).
6. Peter Passel, "The Peace Dividend's Collateral Damage," *New York Times*, 13 September 1992, Sec. 4, p. 3.
7. See Philip Armstrong, Andrew Glyn, and John Harrison, *Capitalism Since 1945* (Oxford: Basil Blackwell, 1991), Chap. 13.
8. One industry that dramatically illustrates the rise of this new competition is the automobile industry. In 1960, imports accounted for under 8 percent of U.S. passenger car sales; by 1988, the share of imports had risen to nearly 30 percent. See U.S. Bureau of the Census, *Statistical Abstract of the United States 1991*, Table 1036, p. 610.
9. A readable statement of this theory is Raford Boddy and James Crotty, "Class Conflict, Keynesian Policies, and the Business Cycle," *Monthly Review* 26, no. 5 (1974): 1-17.
10. Carla Freeman, "From Tourism to Typing: Barbadian Women in the Global Network," *Listen Real Loud* 11, no. 1 (1991): 12-13.
11. Ronald Kwan, "Footloose and Country Free," *Dollars and Sense* (March 1991).
12. The United States has applied considerable pressure to these third world governments to tear down any remaining barriers that limit foreign ownership of capital. The proposed North American Free Trade Agreement

(NAFTA), for instance, would make it possible for U.S. capitalists to own banks, factories, and other businesses anywhere in North America. See William A. Orme Jr., "The Sunbelt Moves South," *NACLA Report on the Americas* 24, no. 6 (May 1991): 10-17.

13. John Miller and Ramón Castellblanch, "Does Manufacturing Matter?" in *Real World Macro* (Somerville, MA: Dollars and Sense, 1992), p. 38.

14. Real wages in Mexico dropped by over half during the 1980s, largely as a result of policies forced on the government of Mexico by the International Monetary Fund, a "banker" to countries dominated by the United States. Since Mexico owes U.S. banks billions of dollars, it has been forced to earn the money to repay the banks by boosting its exports. And if its exports are to be cheap enough to be successful in world markets, Mexico must keep its wages very low. See Orme, "The Sunbelt Moves South."

15. U.S. Bureau of the Census, *Statistical Abstract of the United States 1991*, Table 683, p. 418.

16. Donald L. Bartlett and James B. Steele, *America: What Went Wrong?* (Kansas City: Andrews and McMeel, 1992), pp. 96-97.

17. Samuel Bowles, David M. Gordon, and Thomas E. Weisskopf, *After the Wasteland: A Democratic Economics for the Year 2000* (Armonk, NY: M.E. Sharpe, 1990), p. 126.

18. Barbara Garson, "Respect," *In These Times,* 16-22 September 1981.

19. "Fifty Years of Labor Gains at Risk in PATCO Strike," *In These Times,* 26 August–1 September 1981, p. 14.

20. Alan Finder, "More Employers Seen Using Dismissals to Fight Unions," *New York Times,* 28 September 1991.

21. Freeman and Medoff completed their study before the Reagan administration appointed new, anti-union members to the National Labor Relations Board. The board judges, on a case by case basis, whether such firings violate the law. See Richard Freeman and James Medoff, *What Do Unions Do?* (New York: Basic Books, 1981), p. 232.

22. *Real World Macro,* p. 93.

23. Chris Tilly, *Short Hours, Short Shrift: Causes and Consequences of Part-Time Work* (Washington, DC: Economic Policy Institute, 1990), p. 3.

24. U.S. Bureau of Labor Statistics, *Employment and Earnings,* January 1991, Table 32.

25. Joan Smith, "The Paradox of Women's Poverty: Wage-Earning Women and Economic Transformation," *Signs* 10, no.2 (1984): 298.

26. Benefit data are from Tilly, *Short Hours, Short Shrift,* p. 10.

27. Polly Callaghan and Heidi Hartmann, *Contingent Work: A Chart Book on Part-Time and Temporary Employment* (Washington, DC: Economic Policy Institute, 1991), pp. 6 and 19.

28. Camille Colatosti, "A Job Without a Future," *Dollars and Sense* (May 1992): 9.
29. Richard Belous, *The Contingent Economy: The Growth of the Temporary, Part-Time and Subcontracted Workforce* (McLean, VA: National Planning Association, 1989).
30. Bartlett and Steele, *America: What Went Wrong?*, p. 127.
31. Callaghan and Hartmann, *Contingent Work*, p. 19.
32. Eileen Boris, "Regulating Home Work: The Current Debate," in *First Women's Policy Research Conference Proceedings* (Washington, DC: Institute for Women's Policy Research, 1989), p. 182.
33. Ibid., p. 183.
34. U.S. Bureau of the Census, *Statistical Abstract of the United States 1992*, Table 8, p. 11.
35. Amott and Matthaei, *Race, Gender, and Work*, p. 91.
36. National Council of La Raza, *State of Hispanic America 1991: An Overview* (Washington, DC: 1992), p. 27.
37. In "representation" cases, where the union requests that an election be held so that the workers can decide if they want a union to represent them, the NLRB under Reagan supported management two-thirds of the time, compared to the Ford and Carter boards, which tended to side with unions. See Jonathan Tasini, "Why Labor Is at Odds with the NLRB," *New York Times*, 30 October 1988, Sec. 3, p. 4.
38. Patrick L. Knudsen, "Old Business Nemesis Now Draws Labor's Fire," *Congressional Quarterly Weekly Report* 46 (26 March 1988): 783-85; Henry Weinstein, "Federal Commitment to Worker Safety Criticized by Institute," *Los Angeles Times*, 7 September 1987, p. 3.
39. Lane Windham, "Marchers Demand Justice in Hamlet," *Southern Exposure* (Summer 1992): 4-5.
40. Louis Kushnick, "US: The Revocation of Civil Rights," *Race and Class* 31, no. 1 (July-September 1990). For more on this, see Herman Schwartz, "Civil Rights and the Reagan Court: Challenging the Second Reconstruction," *Dissent* (Winter 1991): 79-84.
41. Maggie Mahar, "Numbers Game," *Barron's* 72, no. 20 (18 May 1992): 16-17.
42. Carl Pope, "The Politics of Plunder," *Sierra* 73, no. 6 (November-December 1988): 52-53.
43. Joel Krieger and Teresa Amott, "Thatcher and Reagan: State Theory and 'Hyper-Capitalist' Regimes," *New Political Science* (Winter 1982).
44. For an exposition of these and other tactics, see William Greider, "The Politics of Diversion: Blame It on the Blacks," *Rolling Stone*, 5 September 1991, p. 42.
45. Alternative Women in Development, *Reaganomics and Women: Structural Adjustment U.S. Style—1980-1992* (Washington, DC: 1992), pp. 18-19.

46. James M. Cypher, "The War Dividend," *Dollars and Sense* (May 1991): 9-11, 21.

47. Isaac Shapiro and Marion E. Nichols, *Unemployed and Uninsured: Jobless Workers, Unemployment Insurance, and the Recession* (Washington, DC: Center on Budget and Policy Priorities, 1991).

48. Isaac Shapiro and Marion Nichols, *Far from Fixed: An Analysis of the Unemployment Insurance System* (Washington DC: Center on Budget and Policy Priorities, 1992), p. 25.

49. See Richard B. DuBoff, *Accumulation and Power: An Economic History of the United States* (Armonk, NY: M.E. Sharpe, 1989), Chapter 7.

50. Doug Henwood, "Did It Work?" *Left Business Observer*, 9 June 1992, pp. 4-5.

51. Lawrence Mishel and David M. Frankel, *The State of Working America, 1990-91* (Armonk, NY: M.E. Sharpe, 1991), p. 71.

CHAPTER 3: SHORTCHANGED: RESTRUCTURING WOMEN'S WORK

1. Jane Humphries, "Women's Employment in Restructuring America: The Changing Experience of Women in Three Recessions," in *Women and Recession*, ed. Jill Rubery (London: Routledge & Kegan Paul, 1988), p. 17. See also John Miller, "Women's Unemployment Patterns in Postwar Business Cycles: Class Difference, Gender Segregation of Work, and Deindustrialization," *RRPE* 22, no. 4 (1990): 87-110.

2. Unpublished data, Bureau of Labor Statistics.

3. Philip Mattera, *Off the Books: The Rise of the Underground Economy* (New York: St. Martin's Press, 1985), p. 38.

4. Colatosti, "A Job Without a Future," p. 10.

5. Mattera, *Off the Books*, pp. 34-35.

6. Comparable earnings data for Latinas were not collected until 1980, at which time they earned half as much as white men. It is likely that the 1970 figure is close to the 1980 figure, considering that the wage gap with white men was relatively constant over the decade for both African American women and white women.

7. Sara Rix, ed., *The American Woman 1988-1989: A Status Report* (New York: W.W. Norton and Co., 1988), p. 395.

8. For instance, between 1985 and 1989 the displacement rate—the number of workers displaced for every 1,000 workers employed—was 6.3 for white women compared to 6.7 for white men; 6.1 for African American women compared to 7.3 for African American men; and 8.3 for Latinas compared to 9.0 for Latinos. See U.S. Department of Labor, Bureau of Labor Statistics, *Displaced Workers, 1985-89*, June 1991, Bulletin 2382, Table 4.

9. U.S. Bureau of the Census, *Statistical Abstract of the United States 1991*, Table 656, p. 400. African American women factory operatives are better educated than whites: only 29 percent lack a high school degree, compared to 36 percent of whites.

10. *Federation for Industrial Retention and Renewal News* (Spring 1992).

11. Joan Smith, "Impact of the Reagan Years: Race, Gender, and the Economic Restructuring," *First Annual Women's Policy Research Conference Proceedings* (Washington, DC: Institute for Women's Policy Research, 1989), p. 20.

12. U.S. Bureau of the Census, *Statistical Abstract of the United States 1991*, Table 658, p. 401. The number of jobs in durable manufacturing fell by 0.8 percent a year between 1980 and 1988 and in nondurable manufacturing (i.e., light manufacturing, such as food processing) fell by 0.2 percent; service jobs grew an average of 2.7 percent. Manufacturing jobs did see some growth in the last half of the 1970s, however, so that over the two decades there was a small amount of overall growth in manufacturing.

13. Because the number of jobs held by women increased more than the number held by men, the percent of service sector jobs held by women increased from 43 percent to 52 percent between 1970 and 1990.

14. Callaghan and Hartmann, *Contingent Work*, p. 24.

15. For Latinas, on the other hand, women's unemployment was higher than men's. While it is difficult to pinpoint the reason for this, it may be because of the relatively rapid growth of Latina participation in the labor force. Although Latinas have the lowest labor force participation rate of the three groups of women, their participation rates are growing the most rapidly. It may be that this growth in the Latina workforce outstripped job creation in the secondary sector, which had traditionally hired Latinas, while discrimination still barred their way in the primary sector—resulting in high unemployment. See Paula Ries and Anne J. Stone, eds., *The American Woman 1992-93: A Status Report* (New York: W.W. Norton and Co., 1991), p. 324. See also National Council of La Raza, *State of Hispanic America 1991*, p. 26.

16. Sara Gould, "Women Building a Future," *Equal Means* 1, no. 2 (Spring 1992): 25-20.

17. Ries and Stone, *The American Woman*, p. 369.

18. U.S. Bureau of Labor Statistics, *Employment and Earnings*, January 1992, Tables 59-60.

19. Freeman and Medoff, *What Do Unions Do?*, p. 153.

20. Cited in Colatosti, "A Job Without a Future," p. 14.

21. Virginia DuRivage and David Jacobs, "Home-Based Work: Labor's Choices," in *Homework: Historical and Contemporary Perspectives on Paid Labor at Home*, ed. Eileen Boris and Cynthia R. Daniels (Urbana: University of Illinois Press, 1989), p. 259.

22. Chris Hogeland and Karen Rose, *Dreams Lost, Dreams Found: Undocumented Women in the Land of Opportunity* (San Francisco, CA: Coalition for Immigrant and Refugee Rights and Services, 1990), p. 4.

23. Marilyn Webb, "Sweatshops for One: The Rise in Industrial Homework," *Village Voice*, 10-18 February 1982.

24. Ries and Stone, *The American Woman*, pp. 347-48.

25. Kavita Ramdas, "Self-Employment for Low-Income Women: A Good Idea in the U.S.?" *Equal Means* 1, no. 1 (Winter 1991): 20-23.

26. Ramdas, "Self-Employment for Low-Income Women," pp. 22-23.

27. Mishel and Frankel, *The State of Working America*, p. 142.

28. Gina Kolata, "More Children Are Employed, Often Perilously," *New York Times*, 21 June 1992, p. 1.

29. Ries and Stone, *The American Woman*, p. 290.

30. Barbara Bergman, *The Economic Emergence of Women* (New York: Basic Books, 1986), p. 147.

31. "Hard Times for Women in Construction," *New York Times*, 29 September 1992.

32. Ries and Stone, *The American Woman*, p. 356.

33. Institute for Women's Policy Research Briefing Paper, "The Wage Gap: Women's and Men's Earnings" (Washington, DC: n.d.).

34. There were two exceptions: in the two blue-collar occupational categories where women have the smallest share of jobs (precision production and craft, and handlers and laborers), women's earnings fell more than men's, widening the gap (see Ries and Stone, *The American Woman*, pp. 361-62). This was because in both these areas, women had so little seniority that their wages were likely to be cut further than those of the men. But since these two occupations account for relatively few women, on average the gap narrowed.

35. Ries and Stone, *The American Woman*, p. 375.

36. Carol Kleiman, "Union Negotiations Pay Off in Number of Pay Equity Victories," *Chicago Tribune*, 24 September 1990, p. 5.

37. Barbara Reskin and Patricia Roos, "The Feminization of Male Occupations: Integration, Ghettoization, or Segregation," in *First Annual Women's Policy Research Conference Proceedings* (Washington, DC: Institute for Women's Policy Research, 1989).

38. Ibid., p. 86.

39. Paul Ryscavage and Peter Henle, "Earnings Inequality Accelerates in the 1980s," *Monthly Labor Review* (December 1990): 8.

40. Ellen Israel Rosen, *Bitter Choices: Blue Collar Women in and out of Work* (Chicago: University of Chicago Press, 1987).

41. Ibid., p. 164.

CHAPTER 4: NEVER DONE: THE CRISIS AT HOME

1. See, for example, Lourdes Benería and Shelley Feldman, eds., *Unequal Burden: Economic Crises, Persistent Poverty, and Women's Work* (Boulder, CO: Westview Press, 1992).
2. Teresa Albanex Barnola, unpublished memorandum from UNICEF, Regional Office for Latin American and the Caribbean, n.d.; cited in Alternative Women in Development, *Reaganomics and Women: Structural Adjustment U.S. Style—1990-1992* (Washington, DC: 1992).
3. Arlie Hochschild, *The Second Shift: Working Parents and the Revolution at Home* (New York: Viking, 1989), p. 9.
4. Schor, *The Overworked American*, p. 37.
5. "Nanny: Confessions of an 'Illegal' Caregiver," *Mother Jones* 16, no. 3 (May-June 1991): 40-43.
6. U.S. Bureau of the Census, *Who's Minding the Kids?* Current Population Reports, Special Studies, Series P-70, No. 20 (1990), Table 7, Part B.
7. Ries and Stone, *The American Woman*, p. 41; Michael Creighton, "Worthy Wage Campaign," *Labor Notes* 159 (June 1992): 16; Isobel White, "Child Care Teachers Organize," *Equal Means* 1, no. 2 (Spring 1992): 14.
8. U.S. Bureau of the Census, *Studies in Marriage and the Family*, Current Population Reports, Special Studies, Series P-23, No. 162 (1989), p. 2.
9. U.S. Bureau of the Census, *Changes in American Family Life*, Current Population Reports, Special Studies, Series P-23, No. 163 (1989), p. 7.
10. Ibid., p. 13.
11. Ibid., p. 14.
12. U.S. Bureau of the Census, *Marital Status and Living Arrangements*, Current Population Reports, Series P-20, No. 450 (March 1990), Table 6.
13. Aaron Bernstein, "Why More Mothers Aren't Getting Married," *Business Week*, 22 May 1989, p. 75.
14. Constance Sorrentino, "The Changing Family in International Perspective," *Monthly Labor Review* (March 1990): 41-56.
15. Kathryn Larson, "The Economic Status of Lesbian Households: The State of the Art." Paper presented at the American Economic Association Meetings, 1992.
16. Patricia Horn, "To Love and to Cherish," *Dollars and Sense* (June 1990).
17. Barbara Ehrenreich, *The Hearts of Men* (Garden City, NY: Anchor Press/Doubleday, 1983).
18. William Julius Wilson (with Robert Aponte and Kathryn Neckerman), "Joblessness versus Welfare Effects: A Further Reexamination," in *The Truly Disadvantaged: The Inner City, the Underclass, and Public Policy* (Chicago: University of Chicago Press, 1987), p. 97.

19. Maxine Baca Zinn, "Family, Race, and Poverty," in *Black Women in America: Social Science Perspectives*, ed. Micheline R. Malson et al. (Chicago: University of Chicago Press, 1990), p. 260.

20. Andrew Sum, quoted in Bernstein, "Why More Mothers Aren't Getting Married," pp. 74-75.

21. Cliff Johnson and Andrew Sum, *Declining Earnings of Young Men: Their Relation to Poverty, Teen Pregnancy, and Family Formation* (Washington, DC: Children's Defense Fund, 1987), pp. 11-12.

22. Vicente Navarro, "Class and Race: Life and Death Situations," *Monthly Review* 43 (September 1991): 3-4.

23. Ries and Stone, *The American Woman*, p. 249.

24. Patricia Horn, "Caging America," *Dollars and Sense* (September 1991): 14.

25. U.S. Bureau of the Census, *Money Income of Households, Families, and Persons in the United States: 1990*, Current Population Reports, Consumer Income, Series P-60, No. 174 (1990), Table 13.

26. Heidi I. Hartmann, "Changes in Women's Economic and Family Roles in Post-World War II United States," in *Women, Households, and the Economy*, ed. Lourdes Benería and Catharine R. Stimpson (New Brunswick, NJ: Rutgers University Press, 1987), pp. 59-60.

27. Arline Geronimus, "Black/White Differences in Women's Reproductive-Related Health Status: Evidence from Vital Statistics," *Demography* 27 (1990): 457-66; Elaine McCrate, "Expectations of Adult Wages and Teenage Childbearing," unpublished manuscript, University of Vermont, n.d.

28. Frank F. Furstenberg, Jr., J. Brooks-Gunn, and S. Philip Morgan, *Adolescent Mothers in Later Life* (New York: Cambridge University Press, 1987), pp. 46-47 and 141.

29. Douglas Martin, "Teen-Agers with Children Also Breed Love," *New York Times*, 12 December 1990, p. 29.

30. Research Committee of the Women and Housing Task Force, "Women and Housing Fact Sheet #4" (Washington, DC: 1992).

31. U.S. Bureau of the Census, *Poverty in the United States: 1990*, Current Population Reports, Series P-60, No. 175, Table 17.

32. Nancy Folbre, "The Pauperization of Motherhood: Patriarchy and Public Policy in the U.S.," *RRPE* 16, no. 4 (1985).

33. U.S. Bureau of the Census, *Money Income of Households 1990*, Table 18.

34. U.S. Bureau of the Census, *Who's Minding the Kids?*, Table 7, Part B.

35. U.S. Bureau of the Census, *Child Support and Alimony: 1987*, Series P-23, No. 167 (June 1990).

36. Sandra Evans, "Putting a Face on Deadbeat Dads," *Washington Post*, 29 May 1991, p. 34.

37. This section is adapted and updated from Teresa Amott, "Working for Less: Single Mothers in the Workplace," in *Women as Single Parents: Confronting*

Institutional Barriers in the Courts, the Workplace, and the Housing Market, ed. Elizabeth Mulroy (Dover, MA: Auburn House, 1988).

38. Author's calculations, based on data from U.S. Bureau of the Census, *Poverty in the United States: 1990* and U.S. Bureau of the Census, *Child Support and Alimony: 1987.*

39. U.S. House of Representatives, Committee on Ways and Means, *Overview of Entitlement Programs: 1991 Green Book,* WMCP: 102-9 (1991), Appendix G.

40. National Low-Income Housing Coalition, *Unlocking the Door: An Action Program for Meeting the Needs of Women* (Washington, DC: NILHC, 1990), p. 2.

41. April Gertler, "Wrathful Tenants Unite," *Equal Means* 1, no. 2 (Spring 1992): 1.

42. *Unlocking the Door,* p. 8.

43. Dena Shottenkirk, "Making Domestic Violence Public," *Ms.* (May/June 1992): 77.

CHAPTER 5: FROM POOR TO RICH, FROM WOMEN TO MEN

1. Cited in Robert S. McIntyre, *Inequality and the Federal Budget Deficit* (Washington, DC: Citizens for Tax Justice, 1991), p. 5.

2. Ibid., p. 8.

3. Author's calculation, based on Mishel and Frankel, *The State of Working America,* Table 2.14, p. 63, and U.S. Bureau of the Census, *Money Income of Households 1990,* Table 6, p. 23.

4. U.S. House of Representatives, Committee on Ways and Means, *Overview of Entitlement Programs,* Appendix G.

5. Jane Gross, "On the Edge of Poverty in California: A Welfare Mother Fears Deeper Cuts," *New York Times,* 11 August 1992.

6. Cited in Teresa Amott, "Black Women and AFDC," in *Women, the State, and Welfare,* ed. Linda Gordon (Madison, WI: University of Wisconsin Press, 1990), pp. 291-92.

7. The data in this paragraph can be found in U.S. House of Representatives, Committee on Ways and Means, *Overview of Entitlement Programs,* pp. 641-44. Even if we take into account the fact that some people may go on welfare several times, over 50 percent of recipients spend less than four years on welfare during their lifetimes.

8. See U.S. House of Representatives, Committee on Ways and Means, *Overview of Entitlement Programs,* p. 643, for a summary of studies of this issue. In addition, there is some evidence that higher welfare incomes, like higher incomes in general, *increase* the likelihood of remaining in school and of attaining higher wage rates, at least for young adults who receive AFDC. See

Martha S. Hill and Michael Ponza, "Does Welfare Dependency Beget Dependency?" Institute for Social Research, University of Michigan, Fall 1984, mimeo.

9. "Children and Families in Poverty: The Struggle to Survive," Hearing before the Select Committee on Children, Youth, and Families, House of Representatives, 100th Cong., 2nd. sess., 25 February 1988, p. 13.

10. The latest survey of characteristics of AFDC recipients (1989) reported educational attainment for 44.6 percent of recipients: 5.6 percent reported 8th grade or less, 15.6 percent reported 1 to 3 years of high school, 17.5 percent had a high school degree, 3.1 percent had some college, and 0.4 percent were college graduates. See U.S. House of Representatives, Committee on Ways and Means, *Overview of Entitlement Programs*, p. 622.

11. "Children and Families in Poverty: The Struggle to Survive," p. 13.

12. Marian Wright Edelman, Testimony before the Subcommittee on Social Security and Family Policy, 20 February 1987.

13. Evidence from welfare-to-employment programs in other states is similarly discouraging. A five-year, eight-state study by the Manpower Development Research Center found only very modest gains in employment or in earnings when comparing participants in welfare-to-work programs with those who did not participate. In particular, the study found that these programs do "not move substantial numbers of people out of poverty." This study assessed state programs built around required job search and workfare programs, rather than programs offering more intensive education and supportive services. However, even these more desirable programs were also limited in their capacity to provide women with adequate employment opportunities. For instance, Illinois' Project Chance placed over two-thirds of its graduates in jobs paying less than $5.01 per hour. (See "Project Chance: Beyond the Hype," The Public Welfare Coalition [Chicago, IL], May 1989.) California's Greater Avenues for Independence (GAIN) program found that over half of participants had educational deficiencies so severe that their immediate job placement was unrealistic. See Manpower Demonstration Research Corporation, *GAIN: Early Implementation Experiences and Lessons*, April 1989, p. 11.

14. Mimi Abramovitz, "Low Income Women's Activism," *off our backs* (November 1990): 15.

15. Cited in Randy Albelda et al., eds., *Mink Coats Don't Trickle Down: The Economic Attack on Women and People of Color* (Boston: South End Press, 1988), pp. 48-49.

16. Paul A. Leonard, Cushing N. Dolbeare, and Edward B. Lazere, *A Place to Call Home: The Crisis in Housing for the Poor* (Washington, DC: Center on Budget and Policy Priorities and Low Income Housing Information Service, 1989).

17. Susanne Paul, "Caregiving: Essentially Women's Work," *Response* (March 1987): 28.
18. Francisca Cavazos and Laura Flanders, "Women Come Together for National Health Care," *Equal Means* 1, no. 2 (Spring 1992).
19. Bergman, *The Economic Emergence*, p. 147.
20. Robert Pear, "Court Nominee Defied Labels as Head of Job-Rights Panel," *New York Times*, 16 July 1991.
21. Gary Orfield and Carole Ashkinaze, *The Closing Door: Conservative Policy and Black Opportunity* (Chicago: University of Chicago Press, 1991), pp. 8-9.
22. Barbara Goldoftas, "Hands that Hurt," *Technology Review* 94, no. 1 (January 1991): 47-48.
23. Randy Albelda, "Aborting Choice," *Dollars and Sense* (September 1990): 16-17.
24. Sidney Blumenthal and Thomas Byrne Edsall, eds., *The Reagan Legacy* (New York: Pantheon, 1988), p. 24.
25. Susan Faludi, *Backlash: The Undeclared War Against American Women* (New York: Crown Publishers, 1992), p. x.
26. Frederick D. Robinson, "Keys to the City," *Southern Exposure* (Winter 1991).
27. Antonio Gramsci, *Selections from the Prison Notebooks* (New York: International Publishers, 1971), p. 276.

Sources for Figures and Tables

Figure 2-1: U.S. Bureau of Labor Statistics, *Handbook of Labor Statistics 1989*, Table 28; U.S. Bureau of the Census, *Statistical Abstract of the United States, 1992*, Table 612.
Figure 2-2: Philip Armstrong, Andrew Glyn, and John Harrison, *Capitalism Since 1945* (Oxford: Basil Blackwell, 1991), Table A-2.
Figures 2-3 and 2-4: Robert S. McIntyre, *Inequality and the Federal Budget Deficit* (Washington, DC: Citizens for Tax Justice, 1991), p. 7.
Table 3-1: Teresa Amott and Julie Matthaei, *Race, Gender, and Work: A Multicultural Economic History of Women in the United States* (Boston: South End Press, 1991), p. 339.
Figure 3-1: U.S. Bureau of the Census, *1970 Census of the Population, Subject Reports: Occupation by Industry*, Table 2.
Figure 3-2: Deborah Figart et al., "The Wage Gap and Women of Color," in Institute for Women's Policy Research, *First Annual Women's Policy Research Proceedings*, May 1989, p. 28; U.S. Bureau of the Census, *Money Income of Households, Families, and Persons in the United States: 1990*,

Current Population Reports, Consumer Income, Series P-60, No. 180, Table 24, and No. 174, Table 13, and calculations by the author.

Table 3-2: U.S. Bureau of the Census, *Statistical Abstract of the United States, 1991,* Table 656.

Figure 3-3: U.S. Bureau of Labor Statistics, *Handbook of Labor Statistics 1989,* Table 28; U.S. Bureau of Labor Statistics, *Employment and Earnings,* January 1990, Table 39, and January 1992, Table 39.

Figure 3-4: U.S. Bureau of Labor Statistics, *Employment and Earnings,* January 1992, Tables 36-37, and author's calculations.

Figure 3-5: U.S. Bureau of the Census, *Statistical Abstract of the United States, 1990,* Table 697.

Figure 3-6: U.S. Bureau of the Census, *1980 Census of the Population, General Social and Economic Characteristics, United States Summary,* Tables 125 and 135.

Figure 3-7: U.S. Department of Labor, Bureau of Labor Statistics, unpublished tabulations from the Current Population Survey: 1990 Annual Averages, December 1990.

Figure 4-1: Sara E. Rix, ed., *The American Woman, 1990-91: A Status Report* (New York: W.W. Norton and Co., 1991), p. 373 [check other refs].

Figure 4-2: U.S. Bureau of the Census, *Current Population Reports, Special Studies,* Series P-23, No. 162, Table A.

Figure 4-3: *Statistical Abstract of the United States, 1991,* Table 84.

Figure 4-4: U.S. Bureau of the Census, *Poverty in the United States: 1990,* Current Population Reports, Series P-60, No. 175, Table C.

Figure 5-1: Nancy Folbre, for the Center for Population Economics, *Field Guide to the U.S. Economy* (New York: Pantheon Books, 1987), Figure 6.4.

Figures 5-2 and 5-3: *Inequality and the Federal Deficit,* pp. 10 and 12. In Figure 5-3, figures are spending changes as a percent of GNP times the FY 1990 GNP.

Figures 5-4 and 5-5: U.S. House of Representatives, Committee on Ways and Means, *Overview of Entitlement Programs: 1991 Green Book,* pp. 620 and 606.

INDEX